# Doing to Done

## PRODUCTIVITY MADE SIMPLE
### ILLUSTRATED FOR BUSY PEOPLE LIKE US

**MIKE WILLIAMS**
with *ART BY KRISTINE YAN*

Copyright © 2021 by Mike Williams.

All rights reserved. No portion of this book may be reproduced-mechanically, electronically, or by any other means, including photocopying-without written permission of the publisher.

Library of Congress Cataloging-in-Publication Data is available.

ISBN 978-1-7358218-9-4

Books are available at special discounts when purchased in bulk for education, business, fund-raising, or promotional use. Special editions or book excerpts can also be created to specification. For details contact our team at specialmarkets@doingtodone.com.

Doing To Done, LLC
350 East Royal Lane
Suite 150
Irving, Texas 75039

doingtodone.com

Printed in USA
First printing August 2021

Art direction, cover, design and illustrations by Kristine Yan (www.kristineyan.com)

*Dedicated to mentors:*

**PAST, PRESENT, AND FUTURE**

# TABLE of CONTENTS

## 01
### WHY
**We're Alone In This Together**

## 02
### HOW
**Design Your Trusted System**

| | |
|---|---|
| Foreword | 6 |
| | |
| Table #3 | 8 |
| The Two Most Powerful Questions | 18 |
| Zoom Out, The Life Map | 37 |
| Small Wins | 47 |
| The Hero, The Foe | 53 |

| | |
|---|---|
| The Four Repeatable Wins | 68 |
| • Sweep It | 73 |
| • Transform It | 91 |
| • Review It | 127 |
| • Do It | 135 |
| The Project Clarity Map | 141 |
| The Role Clarity Map | 166 |

# 03 WHAT

## Build Your Trusted System

| | |
|---|---|
| Build Your Action System | **203** |
| Build Your Storage system | **207** |
| Build Your Keystone Work Beats | **209** |
| | |
| Inaugural Projects | **211** |
| Your First Week | **213** |
| Your First Month | **215** |
| | |
| The Art of Imperfectivity | **217** |

# 04 NEXT

## A Fresh Start

| | |
|---|---|
| Your Fresh Start | **221** |
| Land Of Possibilities | **222** |
| | |
| Thank You | **224** |
| You're invited... | **226** |

| **THE PROBLEM** with most "productivity" systems | **THE SOLUTION** Doing to Done works because it is... |
|---|---|
| TOO COMPLEX | SIMPLE |
| TOO WORDY | VISUAL |
| LAME AF | ENGAGING |

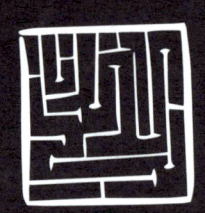

# Foreword

We all choose to fill up our busy lives differently: work, family, fitness, friendships, travel, learning Rolling Stones songs on ukulele...

Like you, I've struggled to find the balance between productive and chill.

But wait—who am I? Why should you care? I'm Stephen Lease, CEO and co-founder of goodr, a fun, successful sunglasses brand. I'll try not to be an infomercial…

This brand was just a dream, and using Doing to Done, personally and company-wide, goodr has grown to exponentially. We sell millions of sunglasses, in thousands of stores, around the world. It feels like I haven't "gone to work" in years.

While becoming a successful entrepreneur, it also helps me be a more present lover, a better friend, a more creative person, and for the low, low price of just $... whoops, took that infomercial thing too far!

I've practiced some amazing productivity methodologies, and most have three problems: too complex, too wordy and lame AF. Doing to Done works. It's simple, visual, fun, and engaging.

Move "stuff" from your mind (doing) to completed (done) so you can be creative, present, and fulfilled in all areas of your life.

Mike Williams is an amazing coach, great friend, and mentor. His system, Doing to Done, will change your life and help you be the best version of YOU, if you let it.

*- Stephen Lease, CEO goodr*

# MIKE'S STORY

# Table #3

It's Friday, October 1. It's a crisp fall night in Vermont. I am sitting with my wife, Arianna, at Leunig's Bistro and Cafe on Church Street in Burlington. We reserved table #3, the table for two near the window. Next to our glasses of cabernet, a candle flickers in a glass orb, as guitar music floats through the restaurant. It's a postcard-perfect scene for our date night.

After a few sips of wine, I hear Arianna say, *"Hello! You there?"*

I wish I had a decent answer. If you could peer inside my head, it was like a storm blowing around and around—emails to send, people I forgot to get back to, and a comment a colleague made that irked me. One big swirling ball of stuff.

Her question made my heart ache; I broke an agreement. I forgot to show up for her.

I was a stressed mess.

ANXIOUS
FLOODED with STUFF.
OVERWORKED UNDER- & OPTIMIZED!!!
STRIVING TO DO Good
Unable TO REMAIN PResent
OVER-WHELM
SLAVE TO MY PHON
READY 2 EVOLVE
STRAPPED 4 attention!
CONSTANTLY DISTRACTED
Successful BUT STRESSED
WORK & LIFE work & Life
WORK + LIFE!
CLUTTERED
CHAOTIC
VICTIM TO A mind
SUFFERING FROM THE BLOWBACK of my Ambition

# Complexity

Life snuck up on me like a perfect storm. I was cruising along, then in just a few short years—single, dating, married, house, kids, promotion, aging parents—I hit rougher waters. I was "successful" but stressed.

Striving to do outstanding work, I suffered from the blowback of my ambition. Anxious, overwhelmed, constantly distracted was my new norm, and it had costs: sleeping less, eating worse, and gaining weight, to name a few. My stress relief was a bag of crunchy, salty tortilla chips I'd pick up at the gas station to keep me company on my commute home.

The biggest cost? I was making agreements and not keeping my word.

I'm not talking big, complex business agreements. I'm talking about the promises I made with myself, my wife, my children, and my friends. *Hey dad, can we play? Yes, but in a bit; I have to work now,* then not show up to play.

I could feel a hollowness building inside me. My actions did not line up with my word. The new levels of complexity were unfamiliar territory, and my old maps didn't work. I needed a fresh approach.

The failed date night with Arianna was my wake-up call.

That's my story. What's yours? Because we all have them.

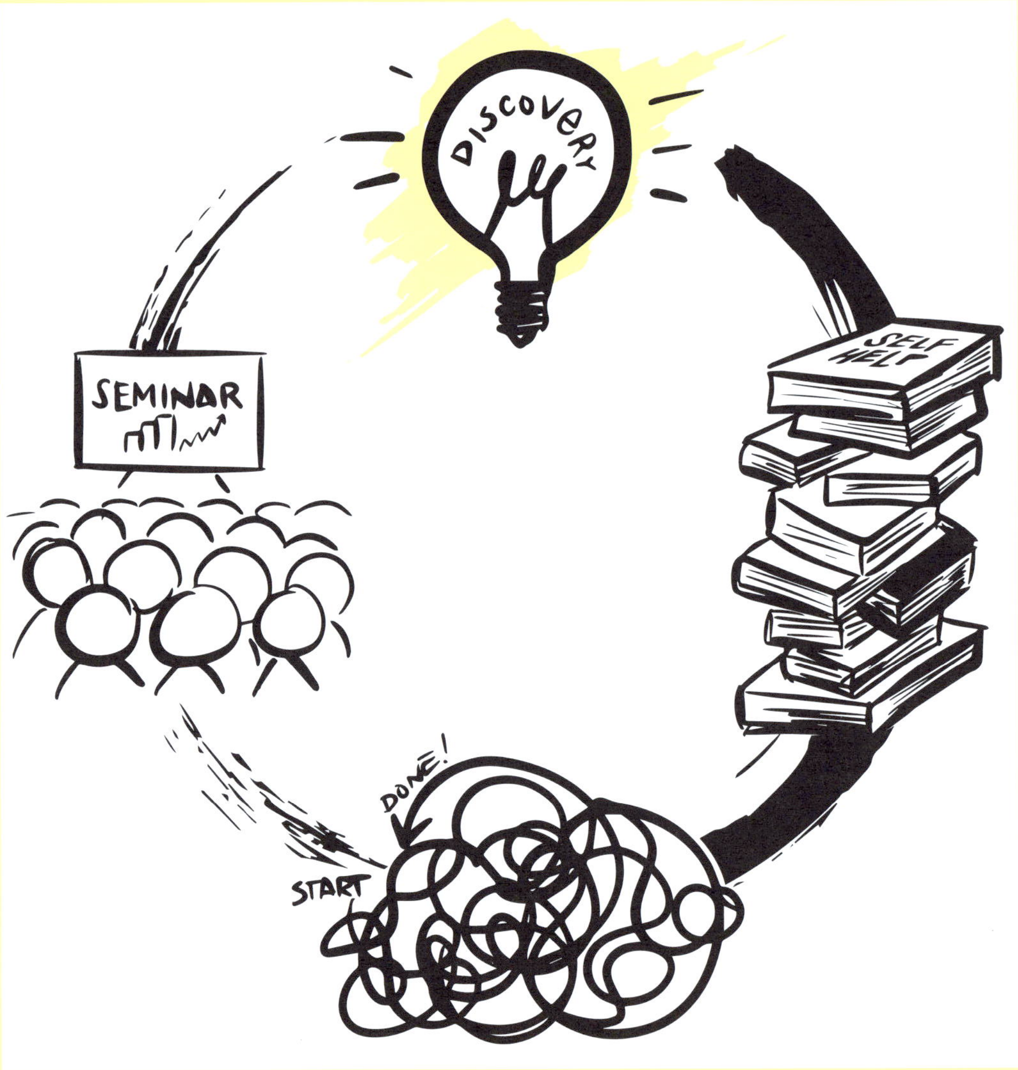

DISCOVERY
SELF HELP
SEMINAR
DONE!
START

# A Better Way

In a twist of fate, my failure as a romantic partner sent me on an unexpected journey and changed my career.

Over the past twenty years I've worked with over 5,000 individuals across many industries, where I learned I wasn't the only one struggling to find a better way.

Neither are you. It seems we are all alone in this together.

Whether through my leadership role at General Electric, my years as the CEO at The David Allen Company, or my time spent as the Productivity Architect (a fancy title for helping people get things done) at Zappos—I noticed one thing time and time again:

### Small wins put joy in life.

Ironically, most of the resources out there are dense self-help books, complex approaches, or snooze-fest seminars.

The coach in me knew there was a better way. I set out to create a path to productivity that was realistic—a simplified, visual, and joyful approach. Surprise! It works.

# Wins on Repeat

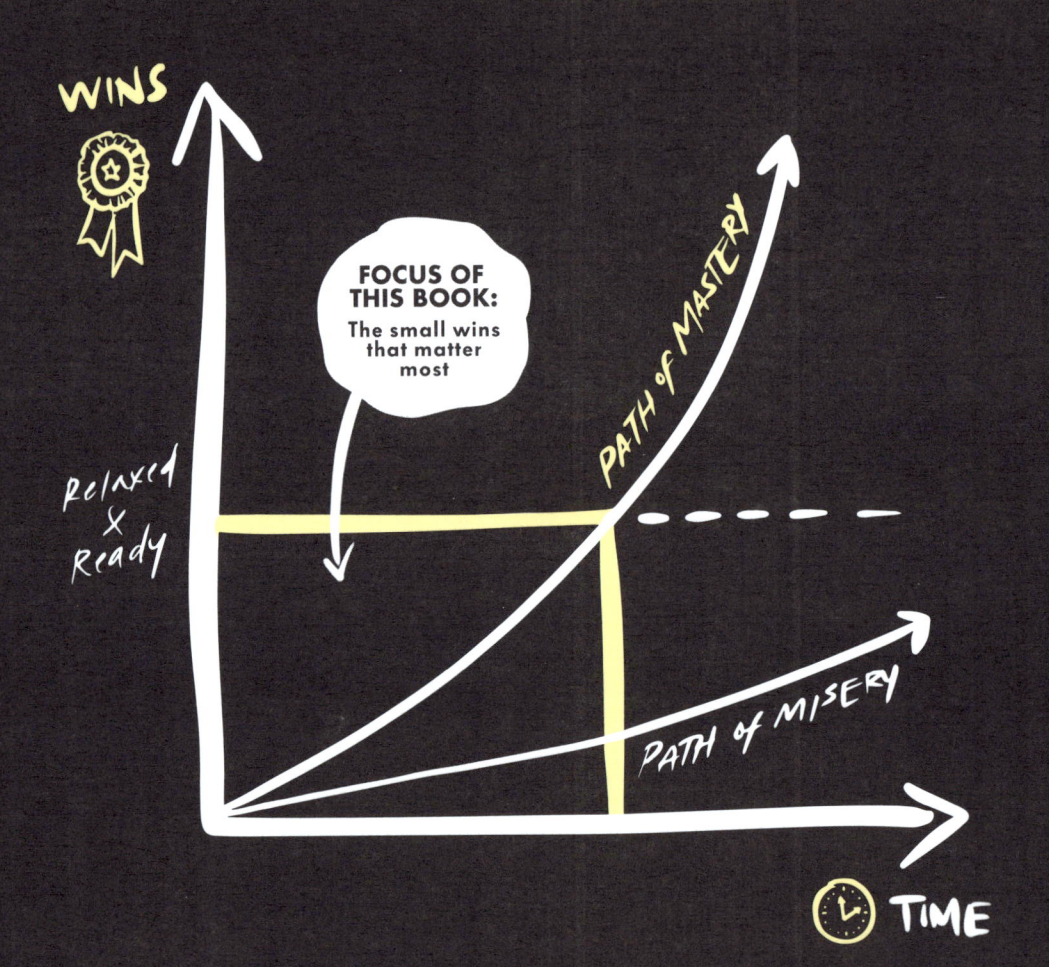

**WINS**

**FOCUS OF THIS BOOK:** The small wins that matter most

Relaxed & Ready

PATH of MASTERY

PATH of MISERY

TIME

# My Promise

Before we begin, I'd like to state my promise to you. I'll help you create small, simple, purposeful wins that lead to lasting impacts in life and business.

## Purpose of this book

To share ideas that will help you produce high-value work with less effort—while reducing stress, increasing joy, and cultivating space.

## Key Difference

I can sum up my key difference in two words: small wins.

This book is simple and packs a serious punch. It's as effective as it is accessible—as impactful as it is easy to implement. I don't promise all of the wins in the world; I'm about quick, repeatable wins by design.

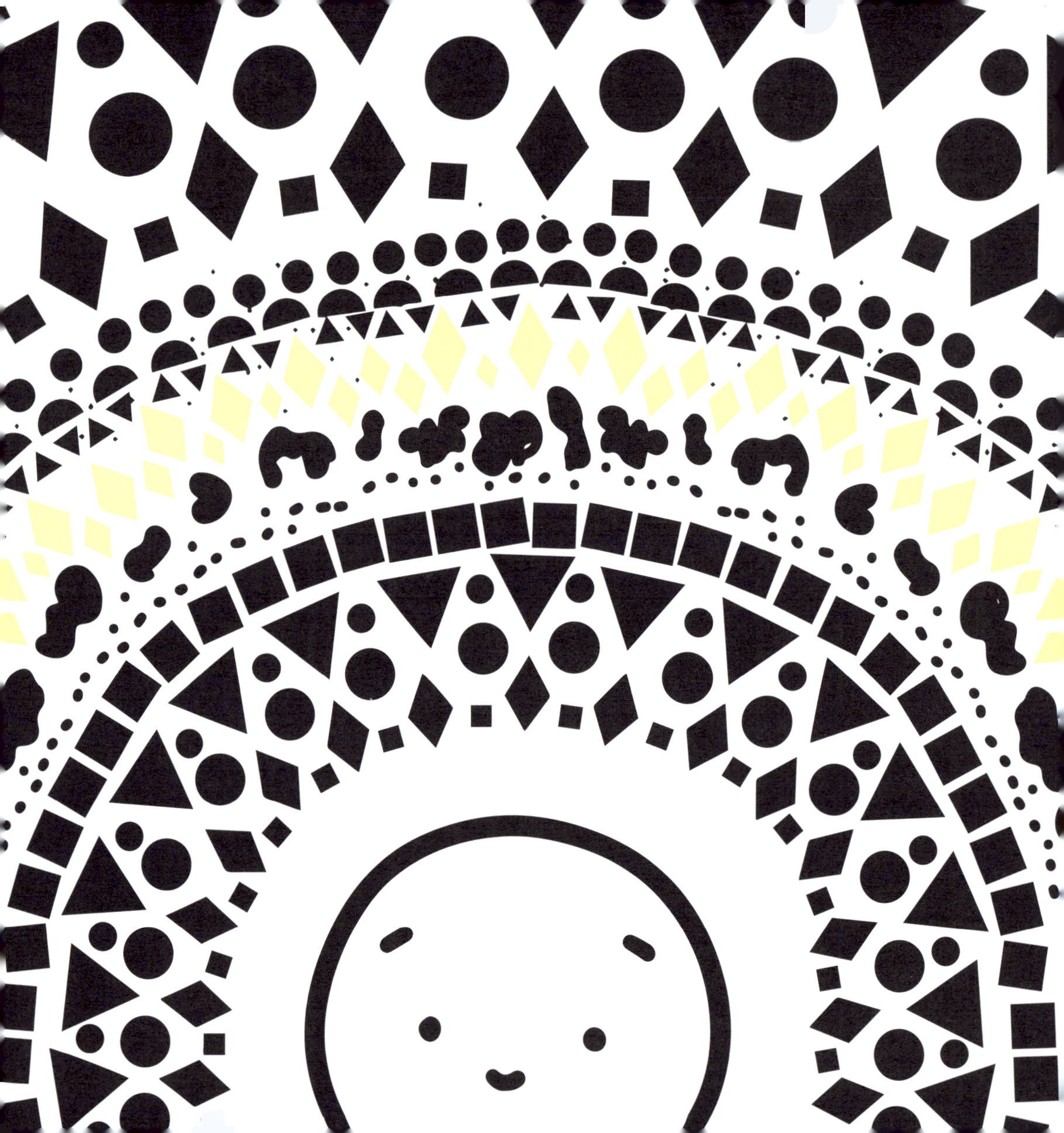

# There's No Better Time Than Now

There's a better way—way better. I'm here to help you tame the chaos and manage the complexities of life with ease—so you can stay relaxed and ready for anything the world throws your way.

Step one? That starts right here.

Turn the page and let me start by sharing with you the two most powerful questions I've asked thousands of leaders.

# The Two Most Powerful Questions

# The Two Most Powerful Questions

If you only have time or energy to read one section, read this one.

Out of all the questions in the universe that I ask people, there are two that stand out as the most potent questions. They work without fail.

I've used them with venture capitalists, rocket scientists, clergy, CEOs, and sixteen-year-olds.

These two questions serve as the starting point for all my coaching sessions (and... this book).

You'll want to grab a pen and piece of paper for this section.

Let's get started with the first question.

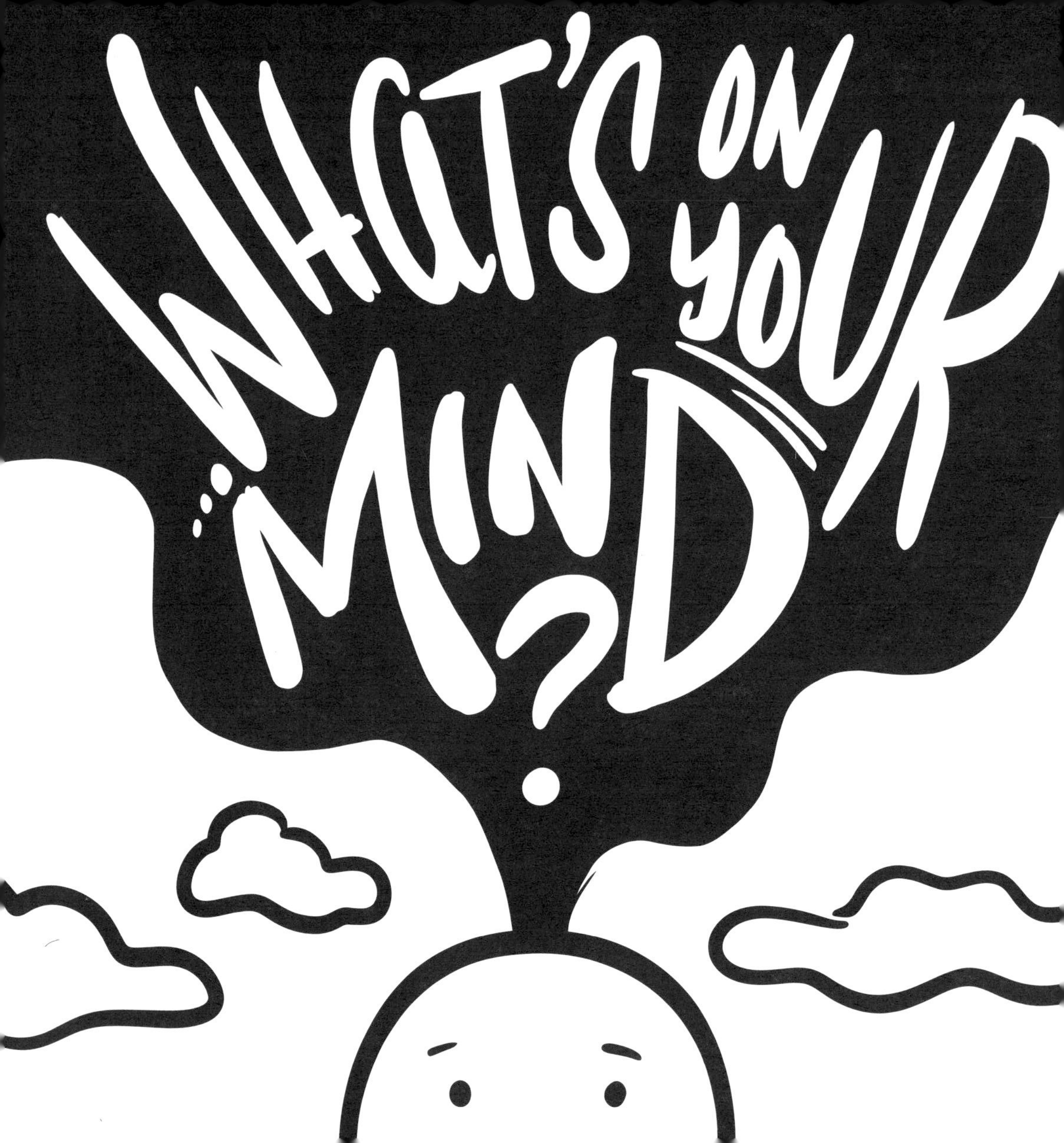
WHAT'S ON YOUR MIND?

# Question 1

Set a five-minute timer on your phone and answer the question:
**"What's on your mind?"**

You don't need to judge or organize your thoughts, just capture what's on your mind. Go for quantity.

Ready, set, *start your timer,* and go!

Here are a few prompts to get you started:

- Any birthdays, anniversaries, or special events coming up?
- Any financial matters have your attention? Do you need a will?
- Any health and wellness items to consider? Any doctor appointments to set up?
- Any people on your mind?
- Any projects to start, finish, or stop?
- *...keep going.*

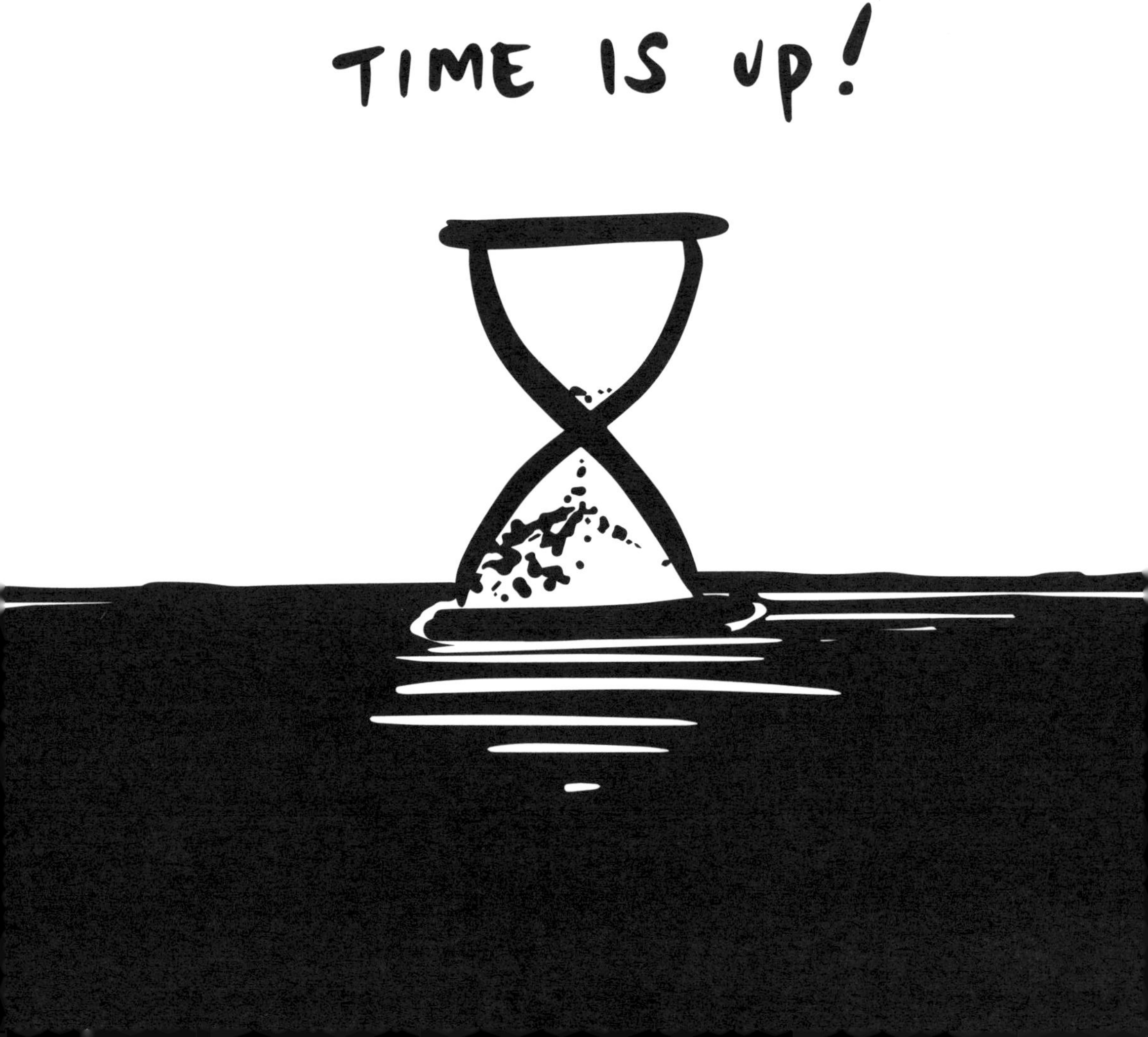
TIME IS UP!

# Time's Up

Pen down.

How do you feel?

Some people feel relief and others feel sad, stressed, or anxious. Maybe you feel a bit of each. It's very natural.

Next, count up the number of items you wrote.

There's a good chance you captured somewhere between ten and fifty items. In my experience, the average hovers around twenty-two.

Let your number serve as a proof point; with five minutes and a piece of paper you captured (insert your number of) ideas. Hold on to your list. It's the starting point for your journey.

For the rest of the book, we use a very technical term for what you wrote. It's outlined in considerable detail on the next page.

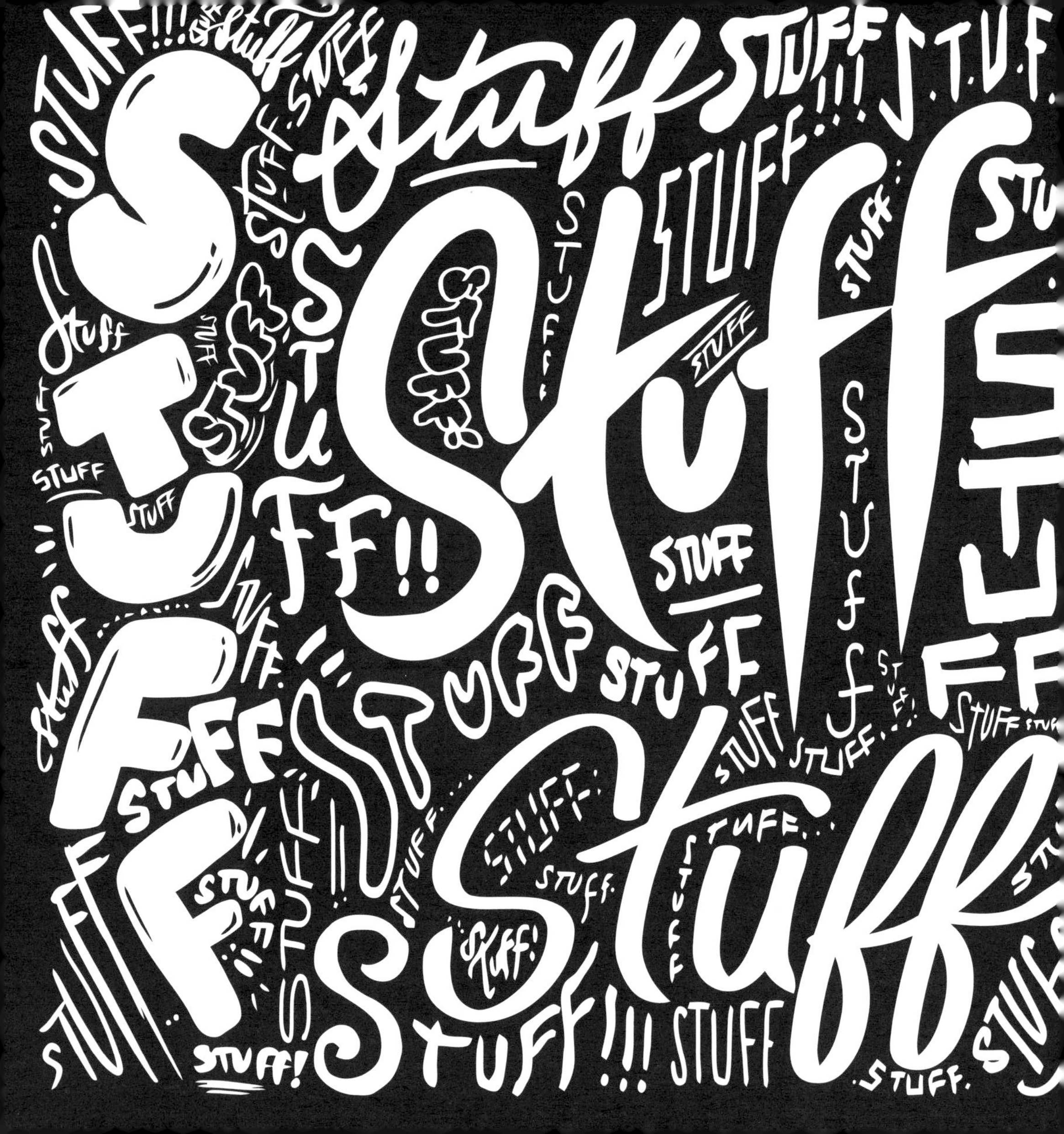
STUFF!!!
Stuff
S.T.U.F.
STUFF...
STUFF
FF!!
STUFF!!! STUFF
STUFF!
.STUFF.

STUFF!
Stuff
STUFFFFFF..
STUFF.
STUFF
STUFF
STUFF!
stuff
STUFF
STUFF
S T U F F
STUFF
S.T.U.F.F
STUFF stuff
STUFF
STUFF
STUFF
S T U F F
STUFF!!!
TUFF!!
STUFF!!!
STUF

# Stuff

We're all fighting the foe that is "stuff"—the clutter, chaos, confusion, and by-design distractions that bounce around in our brain all day.

- That alert you received on your phone this morning from your app(s)...stuff
- The old, outdated clothes in your closet...stuff
- The assignment you got from your class...stuff
- The great idea you had while jogging this morning...stuff
- The notes you took from your last meeting...stuff
- That nagging thought that you keep having...stuff
- A critical insight, a prospect mentioned in a casual conversation...stuff
- The promise you made to your child as you walked out the door to go to work...stuff

Stuff is all around us and is ever flowing like a river.

Managed well, you can ride the currents of creativity and inspiration.

Handled poorly, you might find yourself stuck in a swirling vortex of overwhelm, distraction, and anxiety.

# BRAINSWEEP

- Dentist
- Mom
- Need a will
- Check engine light
- Presentation for conference
- Help Dad
- Email soccer sched. to parents
- Workout
- Eat better
- Date Night
- Sitter for kids
- Check school portal
- Work on budget
- Mulch
- Get paper for printer
- Expense report
- Buy a house?

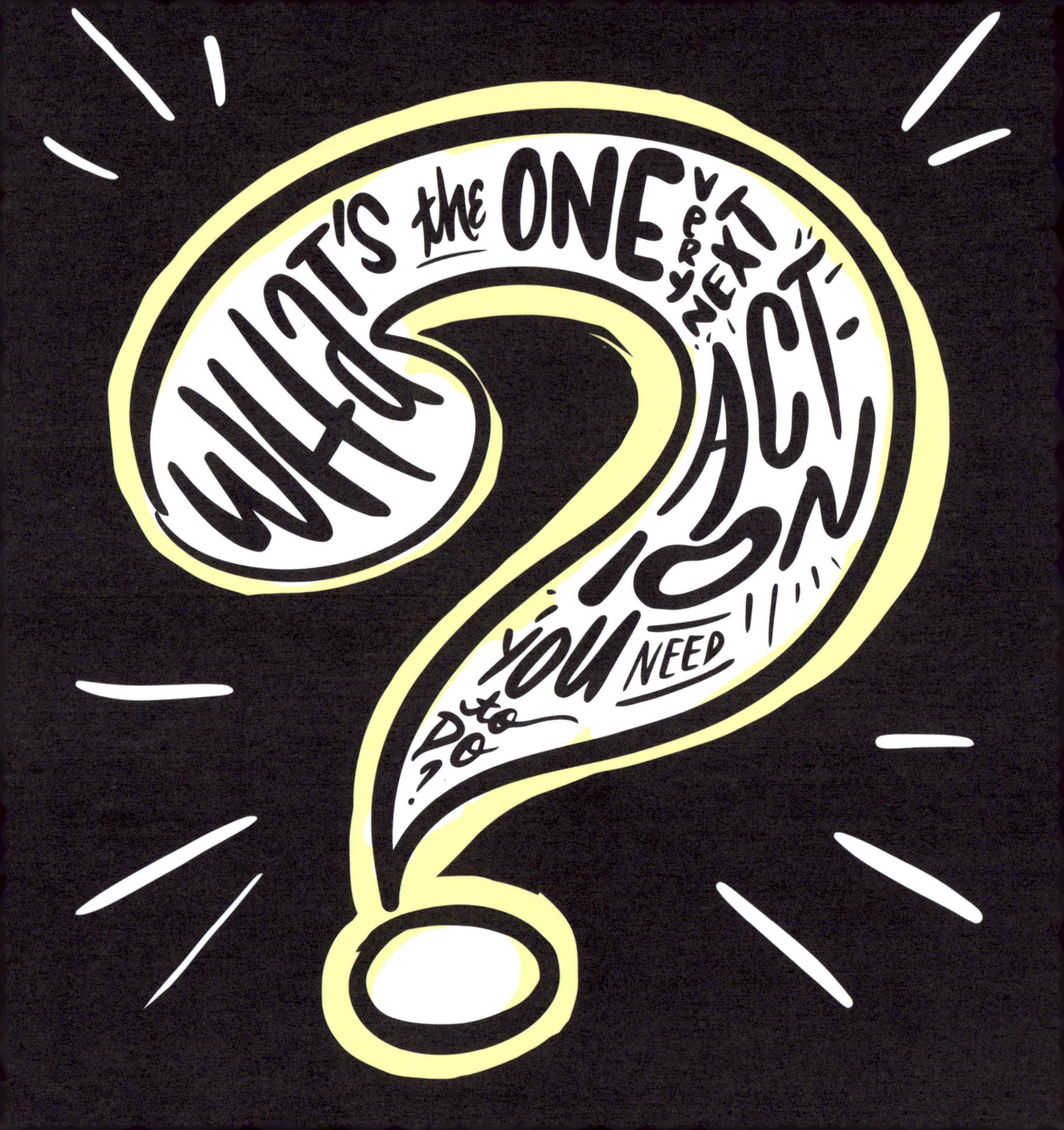
WHAT'S the ONE very NEXT ACTION
YOU NEED to DO?

# Question 2

Circle one thing from your list that you need to handle.

For that one item answer the question:
**"What's the one very next action you need to do?"**

If you put everything else in your world on hold, and this was the only thing in your world to work on, what would you do?

To help you further, let me give you an example.

# One Next Action

Think of the one next action this way: you're the hero in a movie and you need to save the nuclear reactor from blowing up. It's chaotic but you see a manual next to a series of red, blue, and green valves. You open the manual: it reads: *to prevent nuclear meltdown* **<u>turn the red handle clockwise</u>**. You follow the instruction, shut down the reactor, and save the world!

The one next action is a micro-instruction with a specific form:

| Turn | + | Red Handle clockwise |
|---|---|---|
| **(Doing Verb)** | | **(Phrase)** |

Every action you need to take in your life follows the same form. I guarantee it.

| Call | + | Dentist to schedule cleaning |
|---|---|---|
| Text | + | Taylor to meet me at the mall |
| Brainstorm | + | ideas for presentation |

The problem is, most people are not writing the one next action on their to-do lists; it's still in stuff form.

# Doing
# VERB
# +
# PHRASE

# Why It's So Effective

When you write things down, you move stuff from your noisy brain to a quiet piece of paper. You capture each piece of stuff, name it, and pin it down.

- The **<u>one next action</u>** works so well because it is an elegant constraint. It defines a specific goal—all you need is one. It creates clarity and momentum, and prevents overthinking, overcomplicating, and overwhelm.

- The **<u>doing verb</u>** + **<u>phrase</u>** format is a micro-instruction. It's a small statement that helps your brain visualize what to do, like a mini-movie. It is the antidote for procrastination, resistance, and distraction.

The one next action is a love note to your future self.

As I shared at the beginning of this chapter, this is where I begin my coaching but it is not the end. It's the beginning of a journey. Not just any journey, but *your* journey.

# Love Notes to my... Future Self

- Call dentist to schedule cleaning
- Text Taylor to meet at the mall
- Brainstorm ideas for presentation

# Recap

## The two most powerful questions
- What's on your mind?
- What's the one next action?

## Terms
- Stuff
- One next action

## Form
- Doing Verb + Phrase

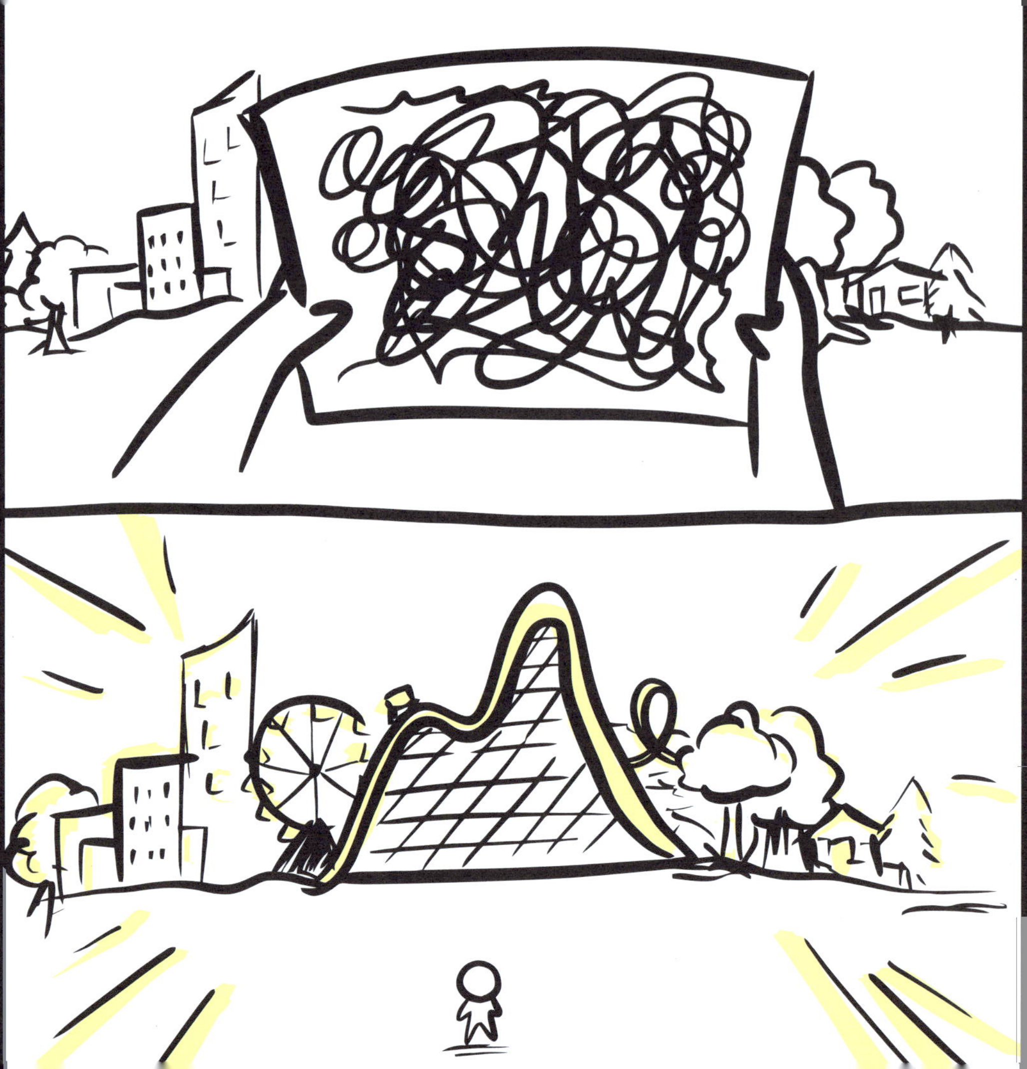

# Zoom Out

To put your list of stuff in proper perspective, we need to zoom out—way out.

- Where did it come from?
- Why does it exist?
- Why is it showing up now?

Every list of stuff has an origin story; let's discover yours.

# The Life Map

Let's create your Life Map—a tool to create perspective and surface bigger questions. It's easy to create and effective.

At the top of a piece of paper, draw an arching line.

Label the left side 0 and the right side 100.

Title the line: *Your Best Life*.

*YOUR BEST LIFE*

We will use this as a proxy for your life. Let's add a few more elements to your map.

# The Current You

Draw a vertical line at your current age. Label this line *current reality*. Think of current reality as the ingredients life gave you to use today. You may wish you had more, but right now this is all you have. It's an ever-present constraint that is a source of creativity.

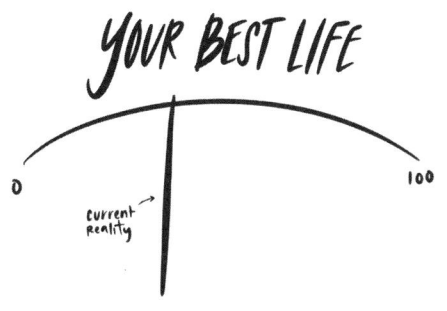

*YOUR BEST LIFE*

0        current reality        100

At the bottom of the line, write *the current you*. The list of stuff you made in the last section reflects the current you set in your current reality.

*YOUR BEST LIFE*

0        current reality        100

the CURRent you

# The Past You

Next, label the left side of your line *the past you*. The events of your past are fixed. The meaning and lessons you can learn are not. As you understand your past, it becomes easier to select more useful actions in the present.

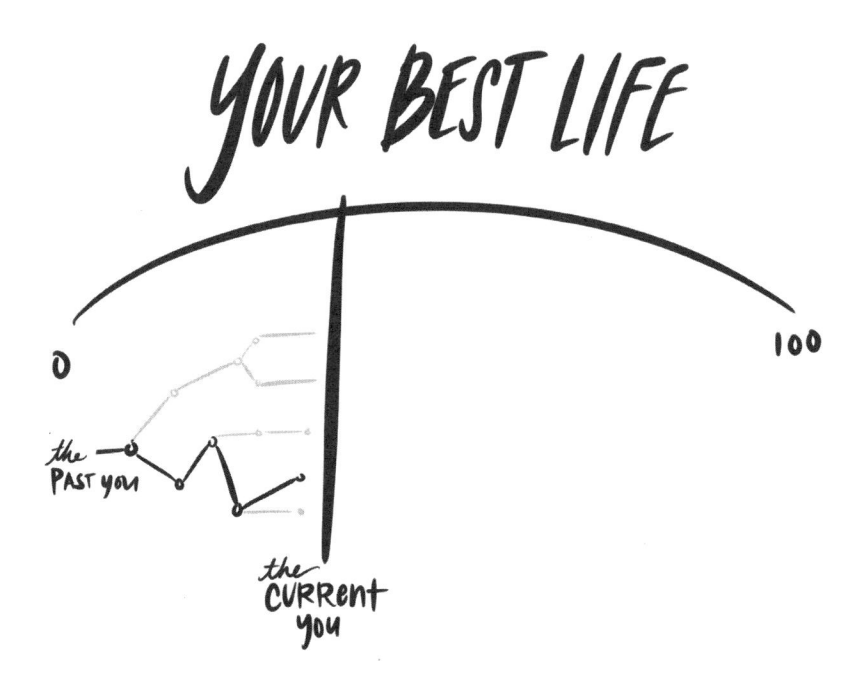

*YOUR BEST LIFE*

0   100

the PAST you

the CURRent you

# The Future You

Label the right side of your line *the future you*.

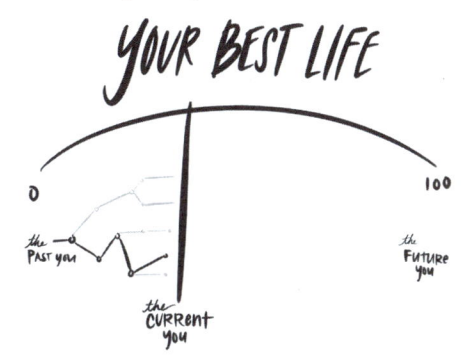

Here's the question we will pursue together: How can the *current you* help the *future you* become the *best you*? At any point in life, you can create a *fresh start*.

# YOUR LIFE MAP

the PAST you

# YOUR BEST LIFE

**Fresh Start TERRITORY**

100 → the Future you

the CURRENT you

"How can the **current you** help the **future you** become the **best you**?"

# Recap

## Tool
- Life Map

## Job it does
- It helps you see life from a broader perspective.
- It surfaces bigger questions (e.g., How'd I get here? Where am I going? Why?).

## Terms
- Current reality
- Current you
- Past you
- Future you
- Fresh start

## Key question
- How can the current you help the future you become the best you?

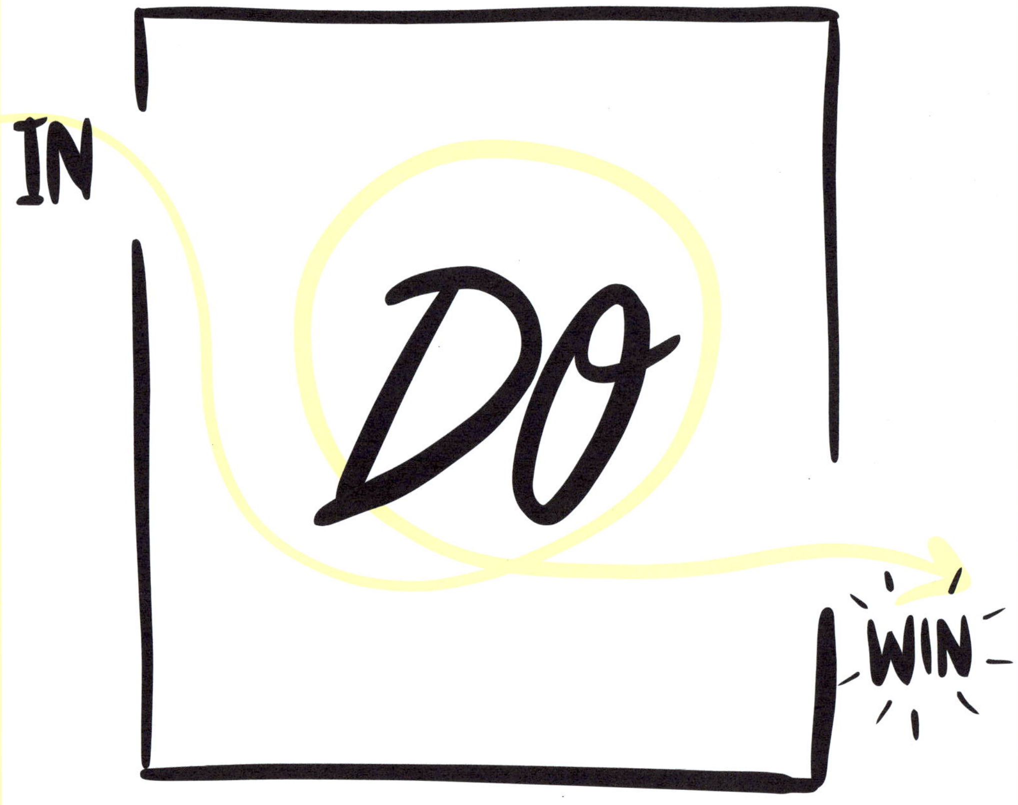

IN
DO
WIN

# Small Wins

How do you win big? Create small wins.

Small wins increase momentum, build self-confidence, and feed your soul. They are the building blocks for a creative and successful life.

Small wins have a distinct form; *In-Do-Win*.

- Enter a space *(in)*,
- Do an activity *(do)*,
- Then stop; exit the space *(win)*.

Magic and mastery emerge as you learn to start and stop an activity. It increases focus and prevents mental drift.

# Work Beats

Small wins fit into *work beats*. A beat is the time you spend in an *In-Do-Win* cycle.

At the beginning of the book, you created five minutes of space *(in)*, wrote down what was on your mind *(do)*, and you stopped *(win!)*. This is a beat. You might spend fifteen minutes *(in)* meditating *(do)* in the morning and stop *(win!)*; this is a beat.

If you're like my clients, 90 percent of your work fits nicely into three types of beats.

**5 MINUTE BEAT** — 5

**15 MINUTE BEAT** — 15

**15+ MINUTE BEAT** — 15 + 15 + 15 + ...

# ONE WEEK

WAKE

SLEEP

# **Fresh Starts**

Each new week holds your work beats. It's fresh-start territory, a blank canvas.

It is here you'll compose your new week, week after week, and insert new beats and let go of old ones.

This is where you'll compose your life and find your internal rhythm, tune, and tone.

# Recap

**Terms**
- Small wins
- Work beats
- Fresh starts

**Job it does**
- Creates momentum
- Creates focus, prevents drift
- Compose your week

**Form**
- In-Do-Win cycles

# THE HERO VS THE FOE

# The Hero.
# The Foe.

As you can see from your Life Map, you're the hero of this story and you're on a journey toward the future you.

Stuff is your ever-present foe.

It's you versus stuff.

Stuff is sneaky. When stuck in your head, it can feel like a...

PARTY in
PSSST..

# the BRAIN

# Party in the Brain

Your brain can get noisy like a room with a raging party. The bass thump, thump, thumping. It's hard to hear yourself think.

At this party, many interesting characters show up. Some invited, some not.

- The spectacular Idea you had this morning on your walk.
- The not-so-helpful Story you keep telling yourself.
- Procrastination is listening to the story about the doctor appointment you've been meaning to schedule.
- A feeling of Shame floats by. "Remember me?"
- In the corner Resistance tells your wonderful Idea, "Yeah, that'll never work."
- Bing! Distraction chases the new alert on your phone like a dog chasing a squirrel.
- And the song you can't get out of your head.

Through the cloudy party chaos, you see a hand waving and hear a small voice, "Pssst..."

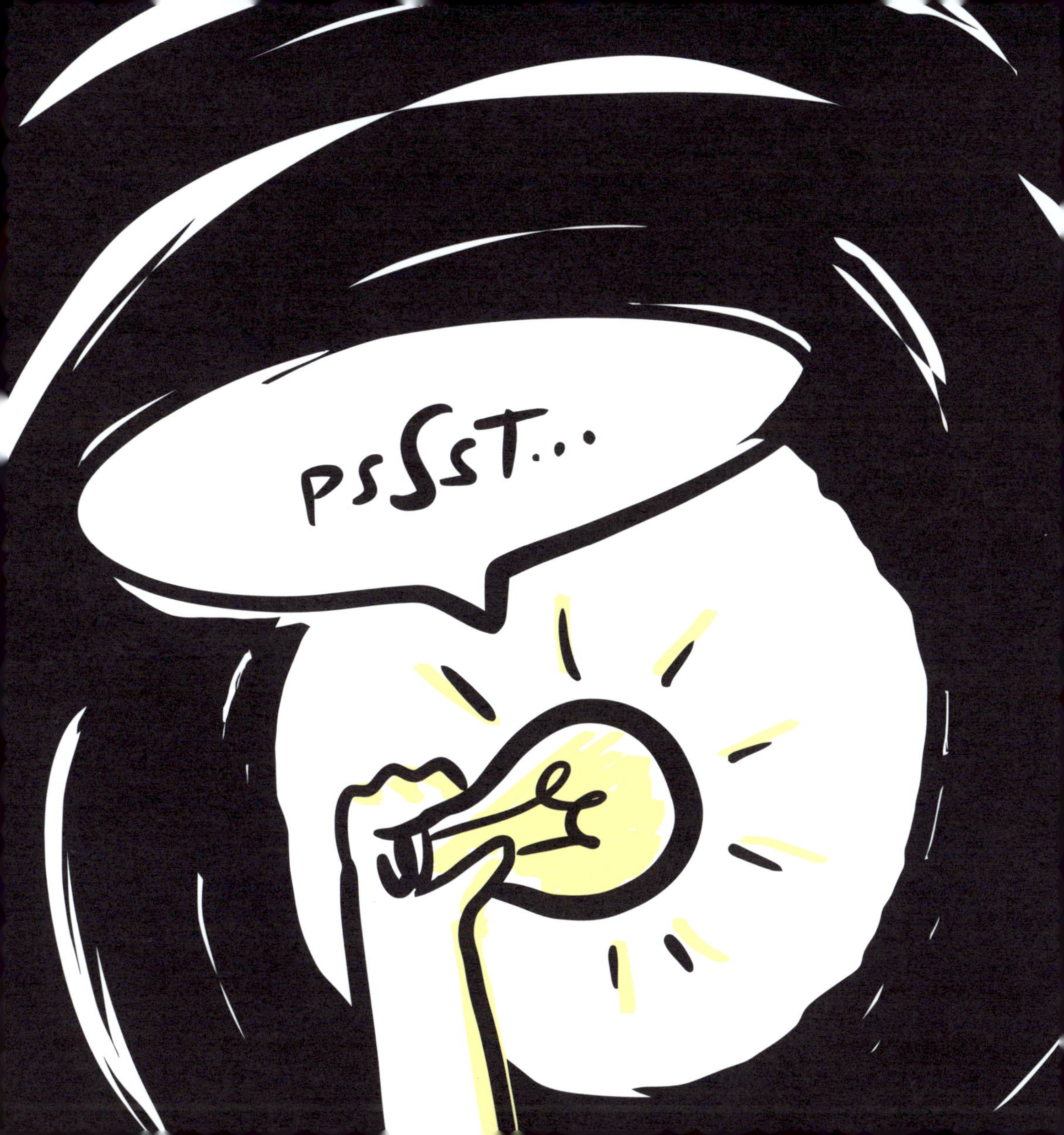
psSst...

# The Small Voice

That whisper you hear is a piece of you waiting to be discovered.

It's too loud to hear what it's saying.

We need a quiet space.

# Empty Your Brain

Party's over. You have thoughts. You are not your thoughts. Show them the door.

One at a time, you can escort your thoughts out of your brain, reduce the chaos, and gain clarity.

When you practice naming what has your attention, you move from the Party in the Brain to...

# CALM

# BRAIN

# Calm Brain

Bruce Lee has a famous saying: "Empty your mind."

When you empty your mind, you notice what has your attention, and some of what you discover may surprise you.

An empty mind has space.

Space for new ideas, space to notice, and space to be.

An empty mind can relax, be ready.

Your brain becomes a calm brain when it trusts you'll handle what it's sensing.

In the next section, I'll teach you how to build Your Trusted System so you'll know exactly how to move from Party in the Brain to the Calm Brain, a critical skill you'll use for the rest of your life.

# Recap

**Terms**
- The hero: You
- The foe: Stuff
- Party in the Brain
- Calm Brain

**Job it does**
- Facilitates the process of de-identifying with your thoughts.

**Key idea**
- You have thoughts.
- You can observe and name your thoughts.

# Design Your Trusted System

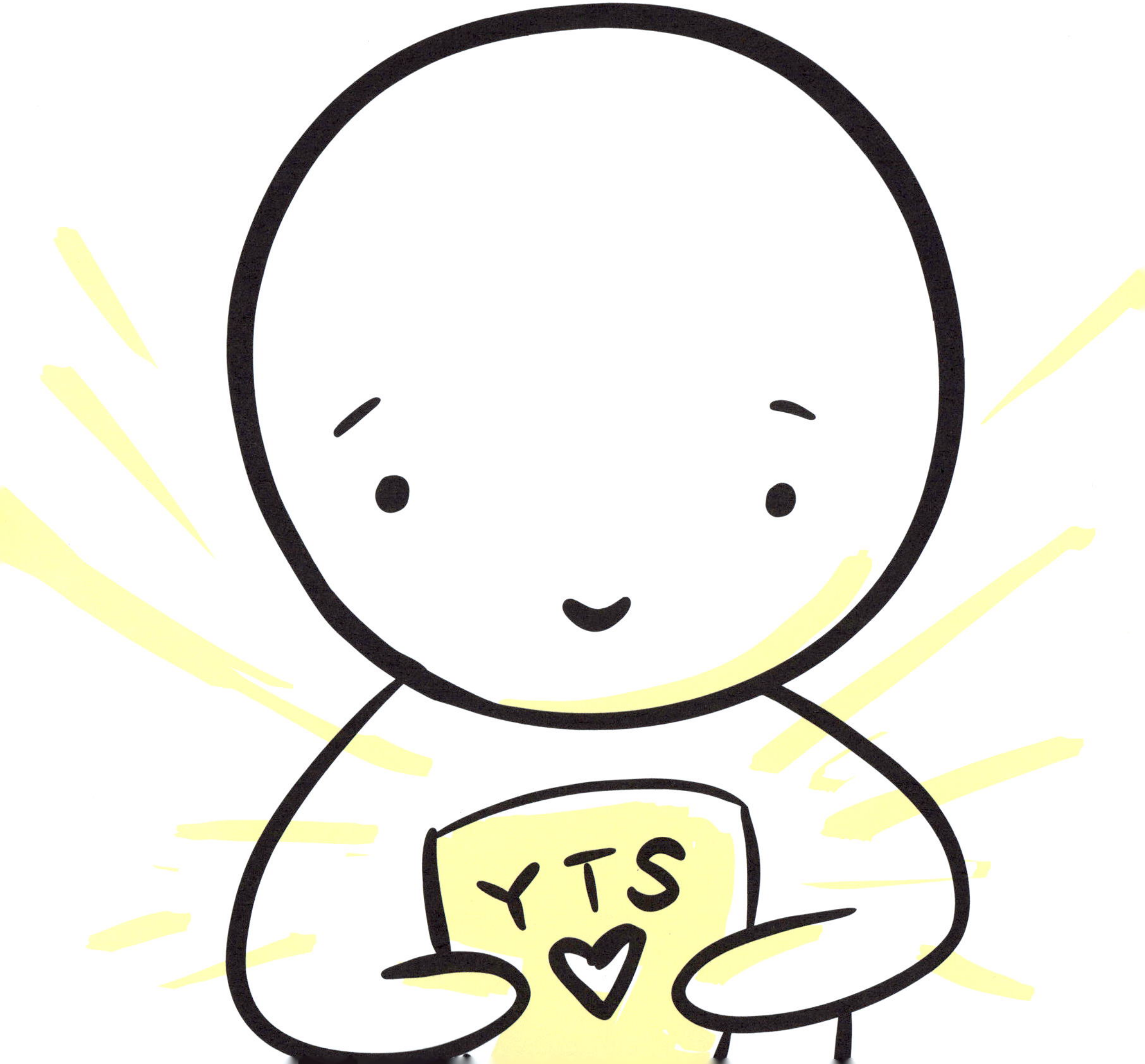
YTS

# Your Trusted System

Stay present, productive, and ready for anything life throws your way.

Call me quirky, but I absolutely love helping busy people like us build simple systems that deliver superior results with minimal effort.

In this section, you'll learn how to build a trusted system. Not just any system, but your trusted system.

- *Your:* You're a one-of-a-kind person. We'll build a system tailored uniquely to your life and needs so you can thrive in all areas of your life.

- *Trusted:* We'll build a system your brain trusts so it can relax. Say goodbye to overload, stress, and anxiety. Say hello to relaxed, ready, and focused.

- *System:* Willpower? Who needs it when you have a system. Get things done using your well-designed trusted system.

Your formula for success—four repeatable wins and two clarity maps.

First up, let's cover the Four Repeatable Wins.

# The Four Repeatable Wins

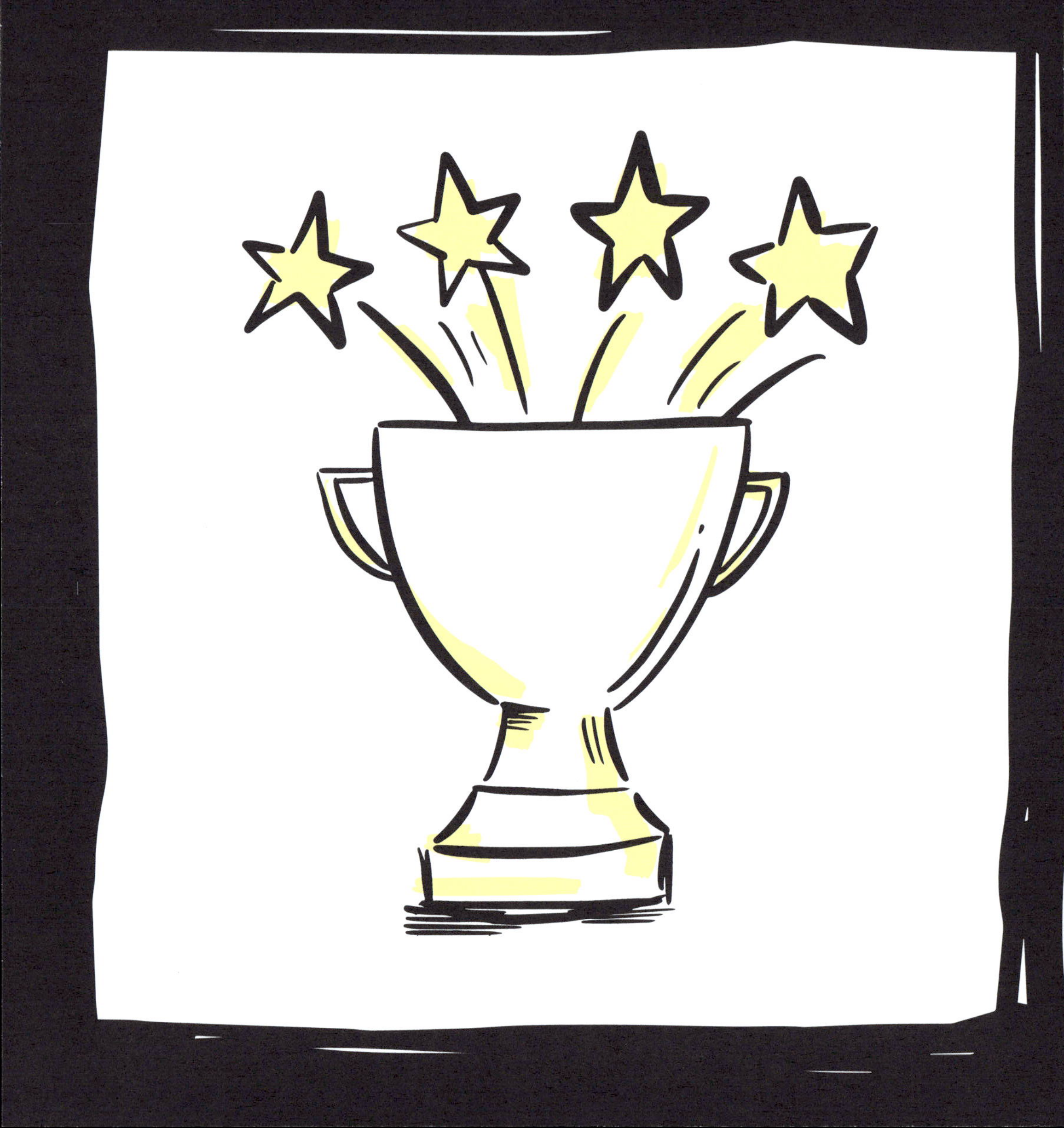

# The Four Repeatable Wins

*The Four Repeatable Wins* make working smarter, living better, as natural as riding a bike.

You'll create small strategic wins that lead to big-time impacts in all areas of your life, for the rest of your life.

With each win, your confidence and productivity soar.

Let's start with the first of the four wins: Sweep It.

# Brain Sweep

## Tech Sweep

## Physical Sweep

# Win #1
# Sweep It

*Sweep It* helps you gather your stuff into small batches so you can tap into some sweet, sweet relief. It's that simple—and powerful.

Small batches of stuff are easy to manage. They set you up for success.

There are three types of Sweeps:

1. Brain Sweep
2. Tech Sweep
3. Physical Sweep

Let's check out each type, starting with the Brain Sweep.

5 MIN. TIMER

# Brain Sweep

Get instant relief with the Brain Sweep.

In less than five minutes, move from a brain full of thoughts back to calm, at ease, and an "I've got this" feeling.

Doing a brain sweep is simple:

1. Set a timer (I recommend five minutes).
2. Answer this question: What's on your mind?
3. Stop when the timer goes off.

*Voila!* A small batch of written thoughts.

Capturing your thoughts on paper is a game changer. Visually seeing your thoughts activates your brain and naturally pulls in more thinking power.

Before we move to the Tech Sweep, let me share Carolyne's story to highlight the simplicity and power of the Brain Sweep.

# Oh No!

At 9:05 a.m. on the dot, Carolyne introduced me to five hundred sales people in her group and took a seat in the front row. I walked on stage and delivered my keynote. Within moments, I had the group engaged in a two-minute brain sweep, offering questions to trigger their thinking.

"Do you have projects to start? Customers that need follow-up? Any birthdays or anniversaries need your attention? Are you waiting for anyone to get back to you?"

Abruptly, Carolyne stood up and walked out. Not seen for the rest of my talk.

Hours later, at the group social hour, while chatting with Don from San Diego about coaching youth basketball, I felt a tap on my shoulder. It was Carolyne.

"You saved my marriage! I've been working nonstop day and night to pull this conference together. I started my brain sweep and realized, 'Oh no! My wedding anniversary is tomorrow!' Perfect timing for your message. Thank you."

One short brain sweep. One celebration saved. Simple yet powerful!

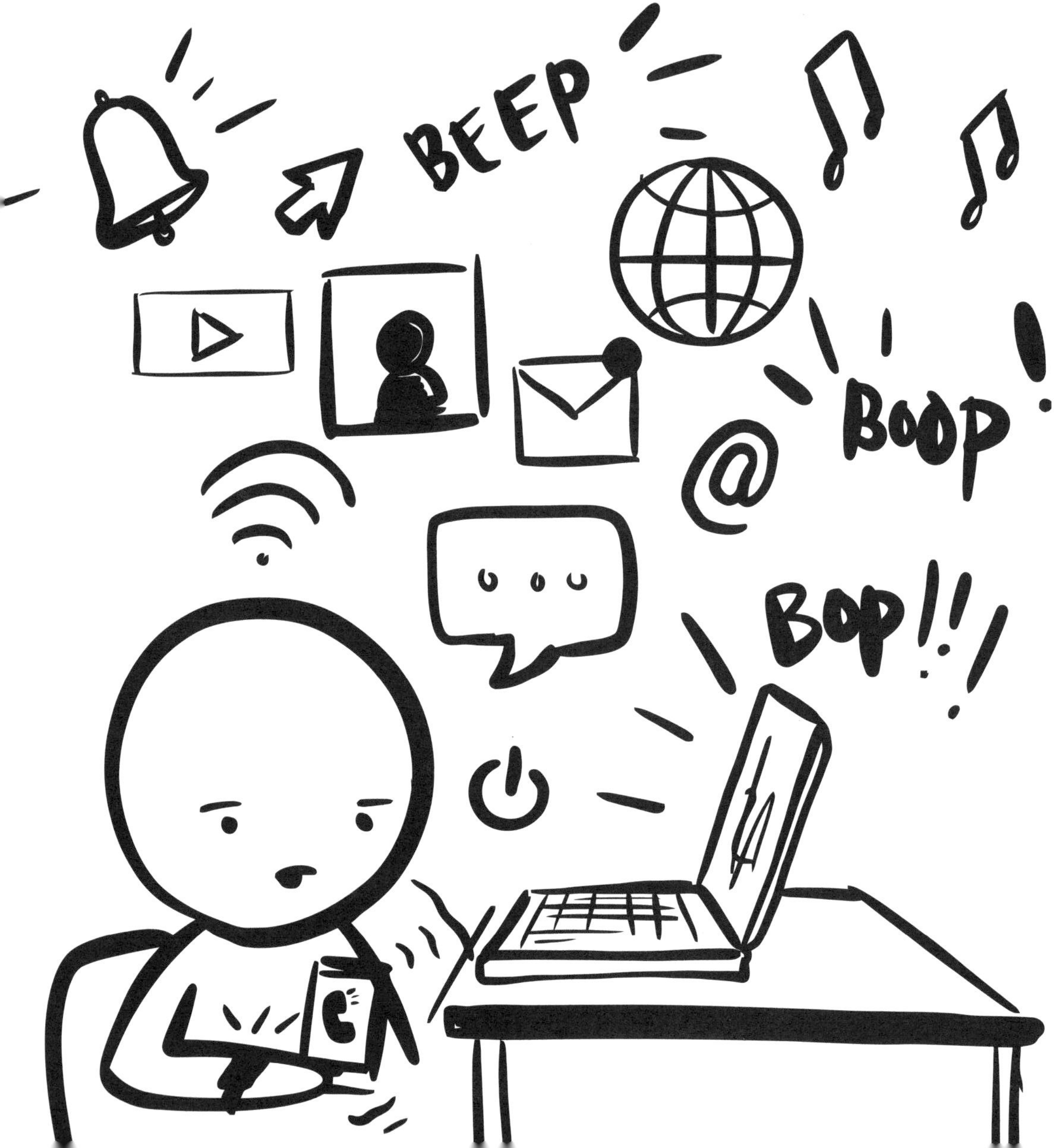
BEEP
BOOP!
BOP!!!

# Tech Sweep

Free up your attention and stay at the top of your game with Tech Sweeps.

Valerie asked, "Can you help me put my phone down so I can play with my son?" And she wasn't kidding. It's the modern-day dilemma. People are constantly on, rarely off. Sound familiar?

It's not your fault. We're contantly distracted—by design. Behind each of the applications on your phone, tablet, and computer is a team of designers, programmers, and scientists spending billions of dollars to get your attention. However, you can change how you engage and take control.

Small tech sweeps of five to fifteen minutes in duration help you batch the time you spend with an application. Instead of checking email or messages at every spare moment, you can break it up into several sweeps throughout the day.

This approach creates defined check-in patterns, keeps you current with your digital channels, and helps prevent habitual checking. Benefits include freedom from your devices, more space to think, and the improved ability to engage and disengage so you can focus on family, friends, and aspects of life important to you. Let me share another brilliant example from my friend Tony.

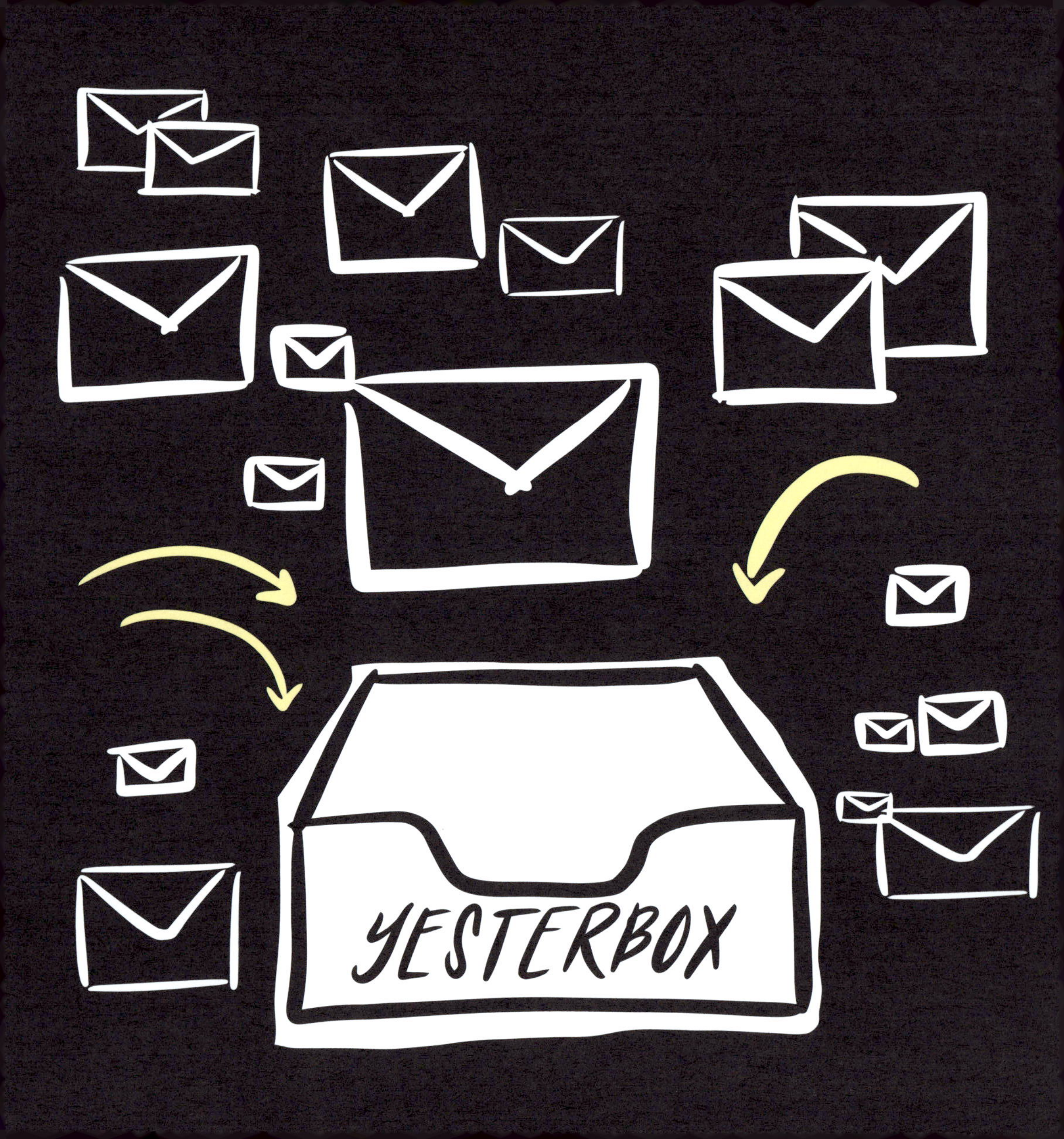
YESTERBOX

# Yesterbox

One of my favorite tech sweep tips comes from Tony Hsieh, the former CEO of Zappos.

You've probably heard of the Inbox Zero movement; maybe you tried it. The idea is you get your Inbox to zero daily. As soon as you do, bing! A new email arrives. It's a frustrating game.

However, you can win the game of Yesterbox. It has one rule: get yesterday's email to zero. Your Yesterbox has a fixed number of emails by design and doesn't grow when you hit zero. You win!

The Yesterbox approach helps you get through email every twenty-four hours. Here's the practice I recommend:

- Sort your email by name; find all the emails you can delete; click delete.
- Find all reference emails; move to a reference folder.
- Respond to the rest.

Use this approach to quantify how many emails you get, how much time you need to process a batch of email, and (pro tip) evaluate why you're getting the email in the first place.

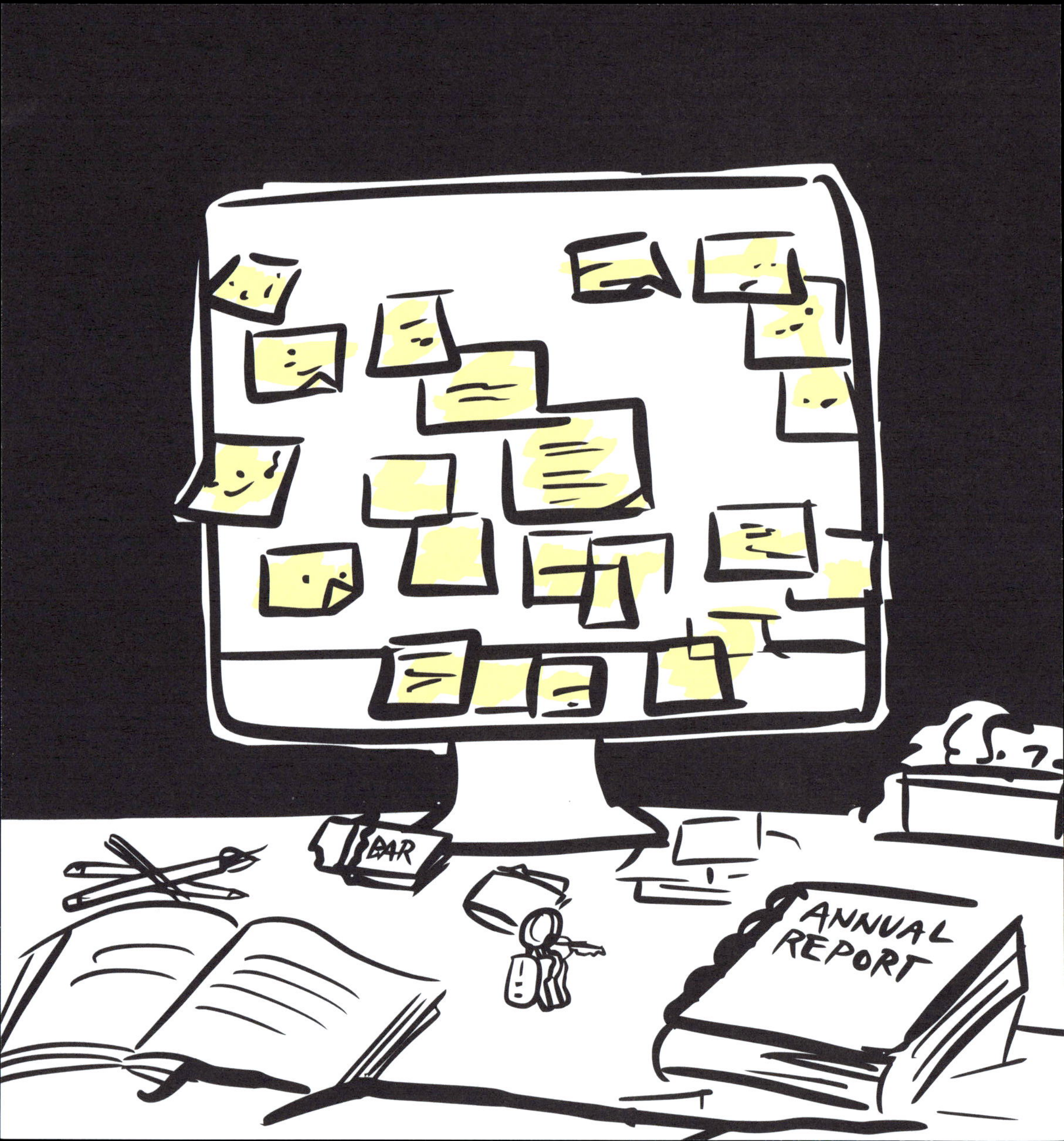
BAR
ANNUAL
REPORT

# Physical Sweep

Keep your physical spaces tidy with Physical Sweeps.

Physical sweeps keep your bags, desk, and room spaces organized.

Like the previous two sweeps, the heart of physical sweeps is small batches.

Handling small batches of physical stuff prevents piles, lost bills, visual distractions, and the stress of always bumping into stuff.

A batch of sticky-notes, today's notes from your notebook, the mail from your mailbox, a basket full of toys—these are all examples of small batches of stuff.

It's easy to handle small batches of stuff.

Let me share a story about my son, Conrad.

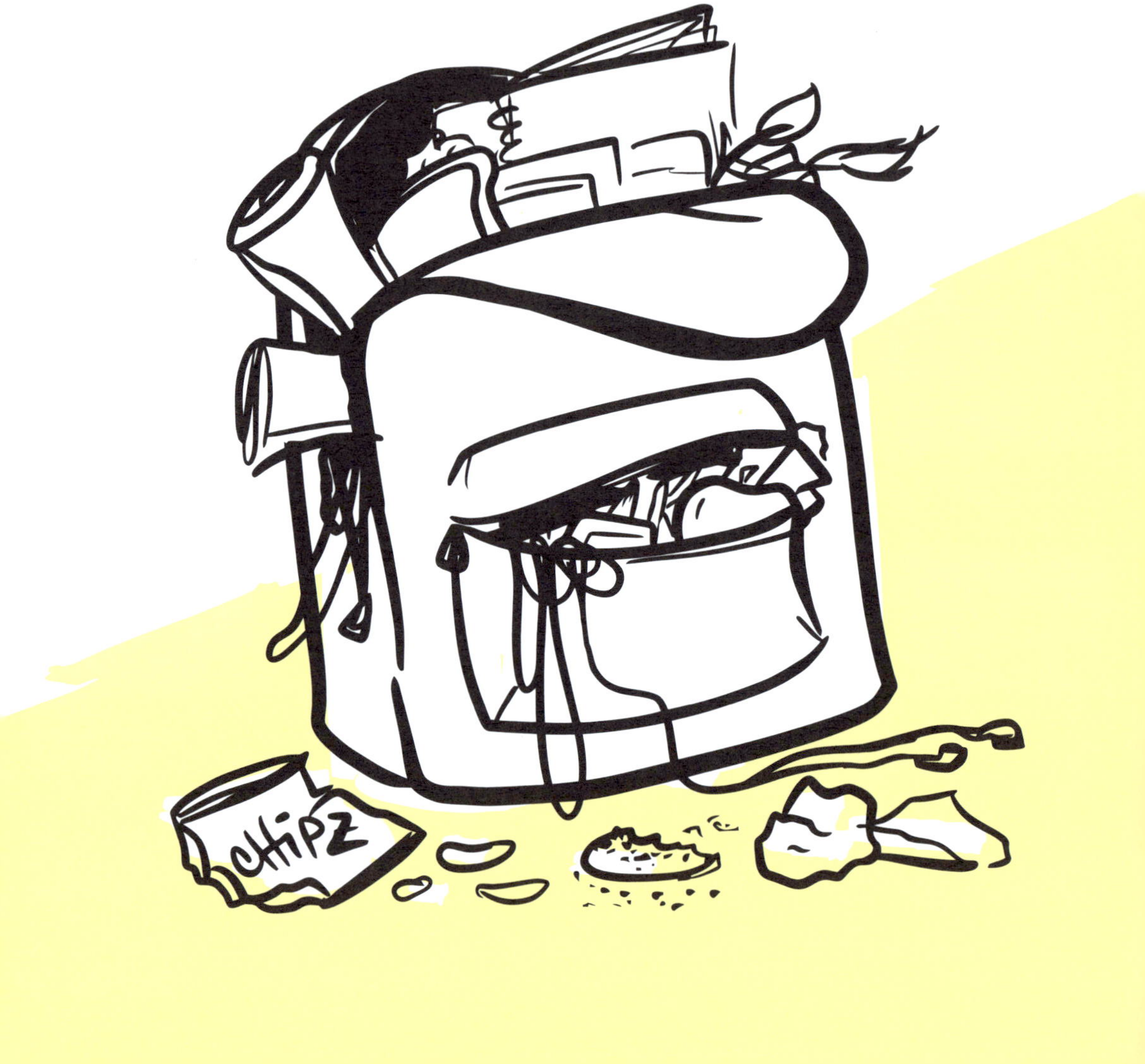
chipz

# Backpack Unpack & Repack

The situation: missing homework, overdue permission slips, homework done but not turned in.

We took Conrad's white Mickey Mouse backpack, unzipped the top, unzipped the front pouch, turned it upside down and shook. It's amazing how much stuff can accumulate after a few trips to and from school.

Books hit the floor, notebooks slid out, homework folders fell. Crushed papers, permission slip for a trip, a smelly gym shirt, pencils, stickers, a stale cookie, and Pokémon cards all fell to the floor into one enormous pile of stuff. I said, "Conrad, this is stuff. We need to tame it."

We set up three piles to organize the chaos: items to place back in the backpack or put in the trash, items that need action. As he repacked his bag, we named this event the Backpack Unpack Repack. We designed a five-minute game he could win. What once felt "big" is now small. It's all about small wins.

Do you have any bags, purses, or briefcases that need unpacking and repacking?

BRAIN SWEEPS — early — BEFO[RE] — MORNING — YOU [start] WORK

Late Morning

LATE AFTERNOON SWEEP

Commo[n]

end of DAY SWEEP

MSGS — APPS — SWPS

PRE-MEETING SWEEP
POST-MEETING SWEEP
WALKING BRAIN SWEEP

TECH SWEEPS

VOICE SWEEP
MAIL
EMAIL @ SWEEP

# SWEEPS

- BAG SWEEP
- BACKPACK SWEEP
- BUILDING SWEEP
- PHYSICAL SWEEPS
- ROOM SWEEP
- STICKY NOTE SWEEP
- MAIL SWEEP
- NOTEBOOK SWEEP
- MEDIA SWEEP
- LAUNDRY SWEEP
- PORTAL SWEEP
- CAR SWEEP
- PURSE SWEEP
- DESK SWEEP
- KITCHEN SWEEP

"GATHER YOUR STUFF INTO SMALL BATCHES, SO YOU CAN TAP INTO SOME SWEET, SWEET RELIEF."

# Recap

**Terms**
- Brain Sweep
- Tech Sweep
- Physical Sweep

**Job it does**
- Sweeps help you gather stuff into small batches using minimal time and energy.
- Sweeps are radically simple and efficient; 5-minute and 15-minute sweeps handle almost everything.

**Key idea**
- Get instant relief, free up your attention, and keep your spaces tidy using sweeps.

Let's bring your Brain Sweep to the next step: Transform It.

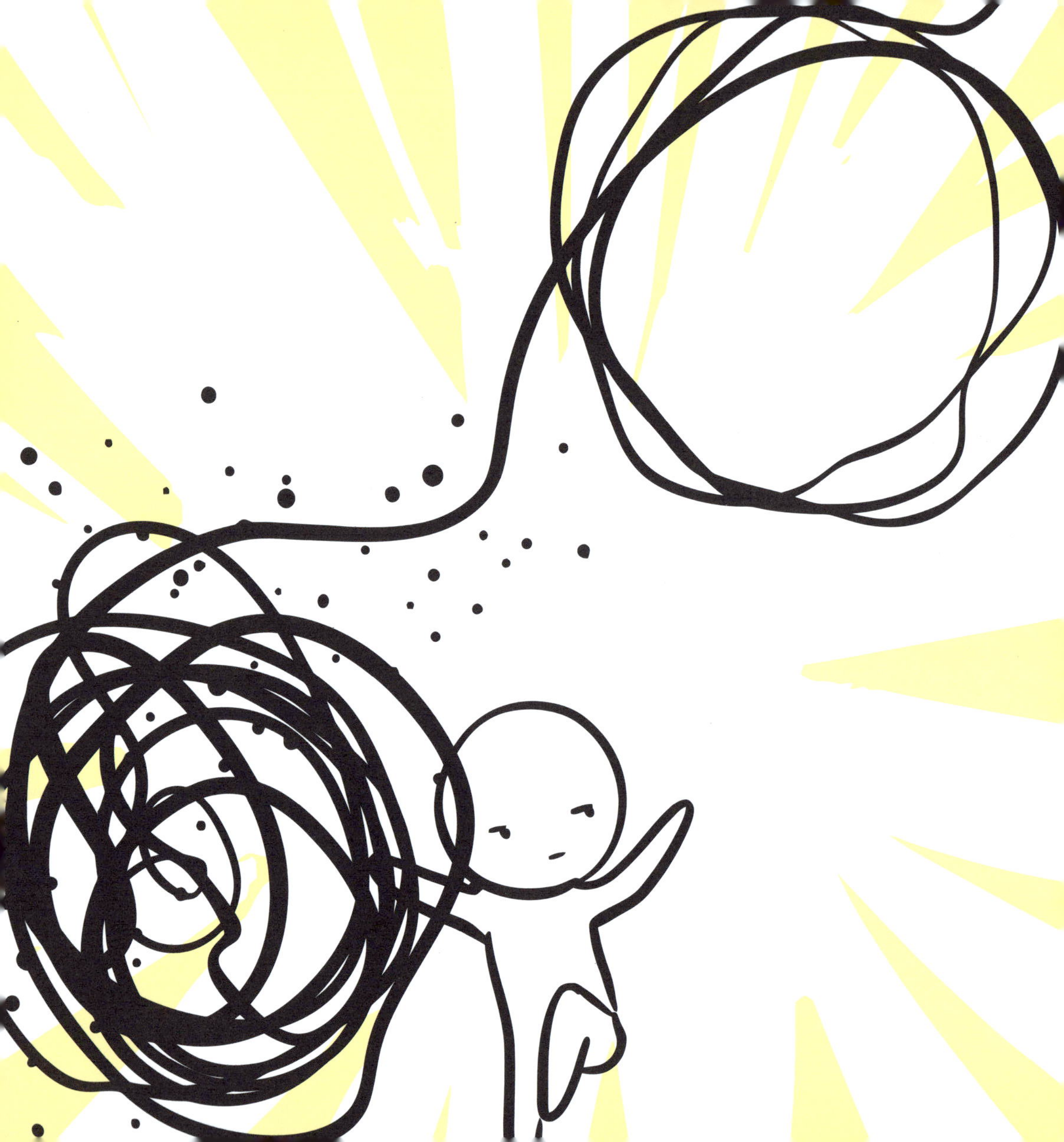

# Win #2
# Transform It

The Transform It step puts amazing clarity into your life.

You come face to face with the stuff you gathered into small batches: the brain sweep, the tech sweep, the physical sweep.

Like a master martial artist facing a foe, you decide what to do with each piece of stuff; then it ceases to exist. You win. You transform your stuff into action elements and storage elements, which you will use to build your Action System and Storage System.

It is a powerful step that will surprise and delight you.

I'll use my brain sweep from earlier to show you how it works. Follow along with yours.

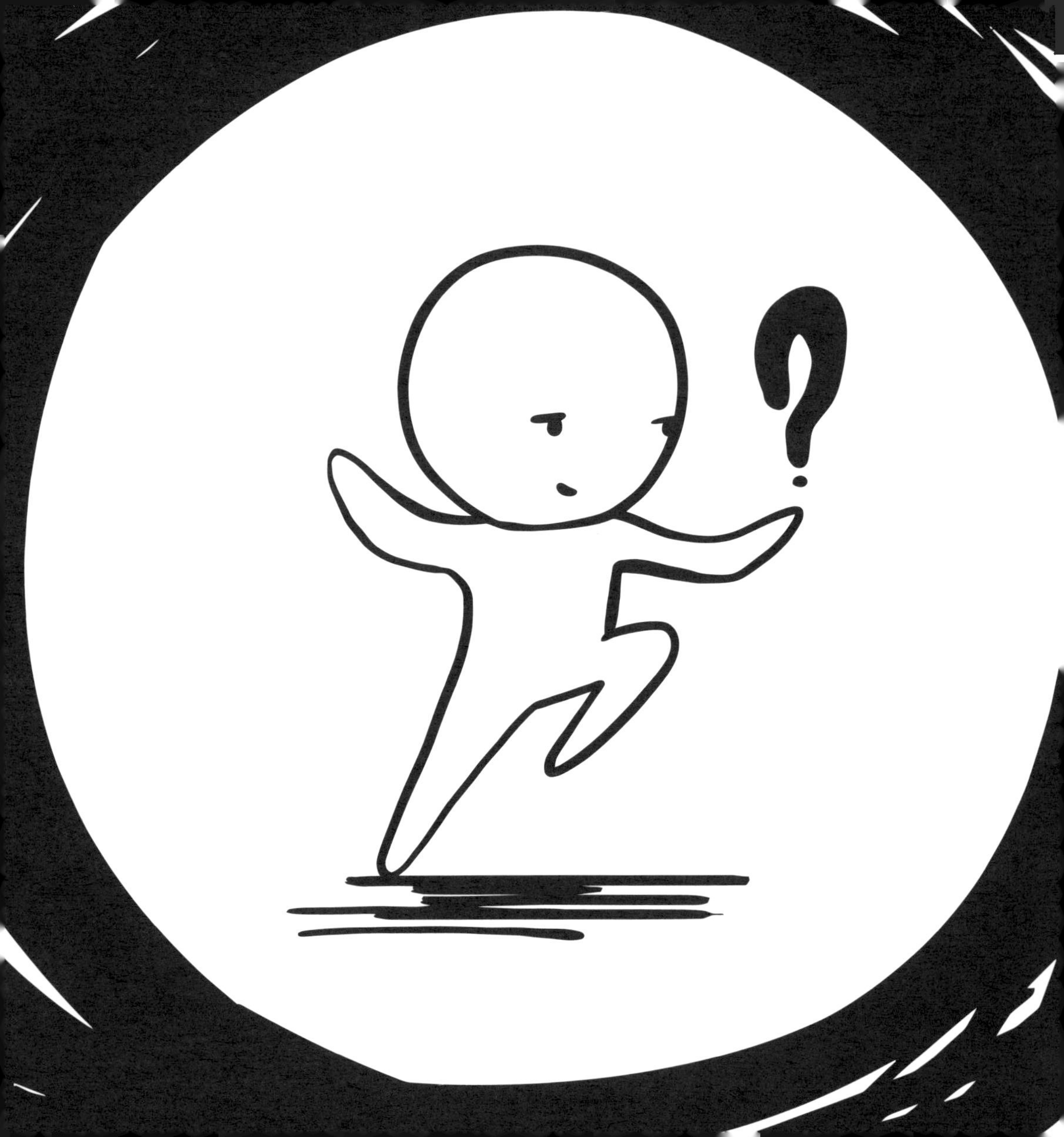

# The Question Is Your Coach

Simple questions power the Transform It step.

You can think of each question as your personal coach guiding you through the process.

After a few rounds of practice, the questions will feel second nature. You'll discover their form, rhythm, and cadence. You'll create clarity with ease.

I liken it to a martial art of the highest order. I often refer to the Transform It step as the Hero Flow.

It's where you unpack and discover what you (the hero) are doing—and why.

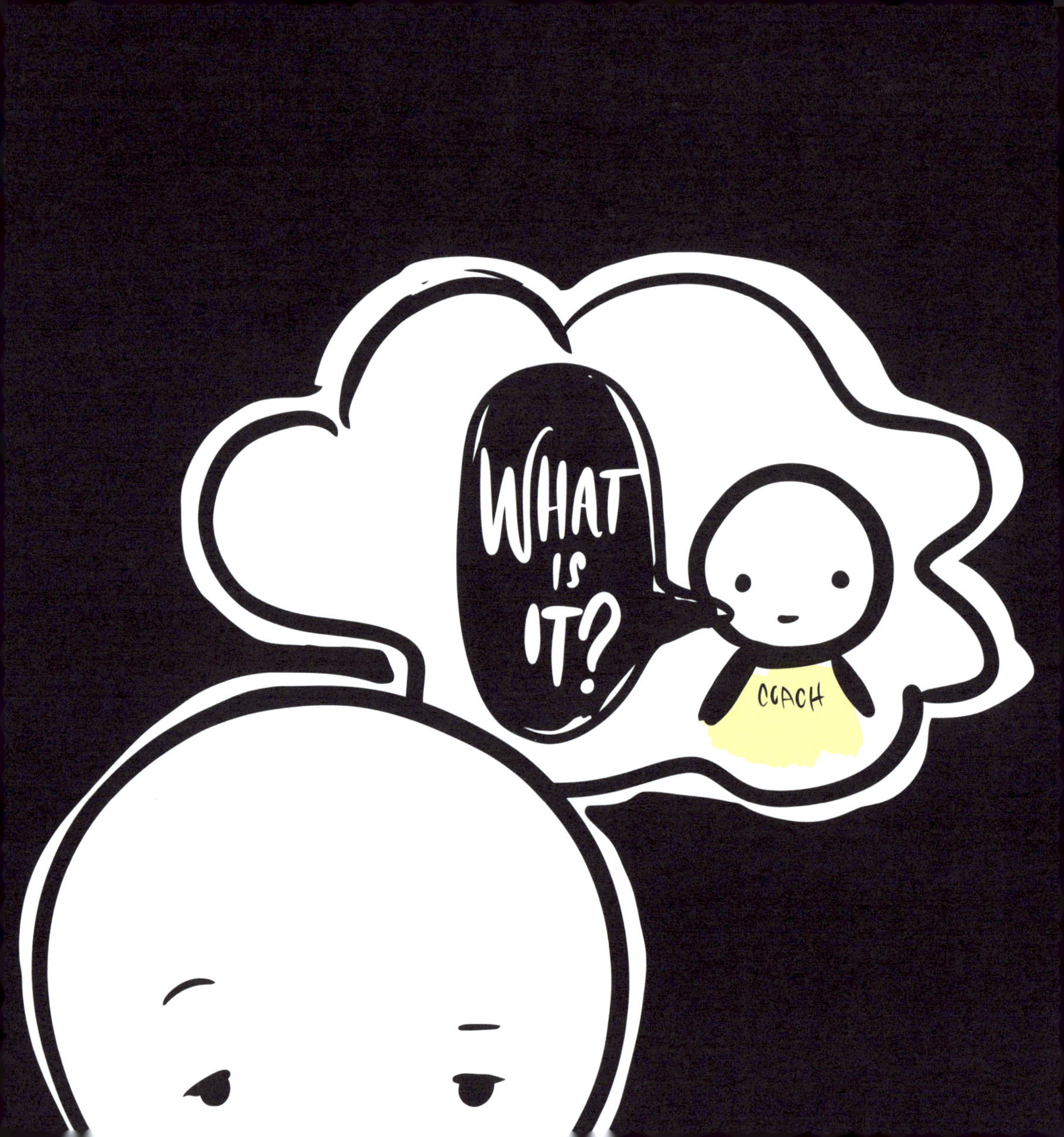
WHAT IS IT?
COACH

# What Is It?

The first step is to select a piece of stuff from your list, then ask, "What is it?"

This question brings forth the meaning behind your piece of stuff.

For example, you may have *light bulb* on your list. It may have a simple meaning for you: *I need to change the light bulb in the kitchen.* That's straightforward.

Or you might have a simple word like "mom" on your list pointing to something that's more complex. That could have many meanings: *call Mom to check in, celebrate Mom's 50th birthday, mend relationship with Mom, figure out living arrangements for Mom, or figure out Mother's Day plans.*

Let's follow a piece of stuff through the process:

- The first piece of stuff on my brain sweep list: *dentist.*
- What is it?
- *Well, I chipped my molar eating some popcorn and I need to get it fixed.*

With that established, I'm ready for the next question in the flow. Select an item from your list that needs action and turn the page.

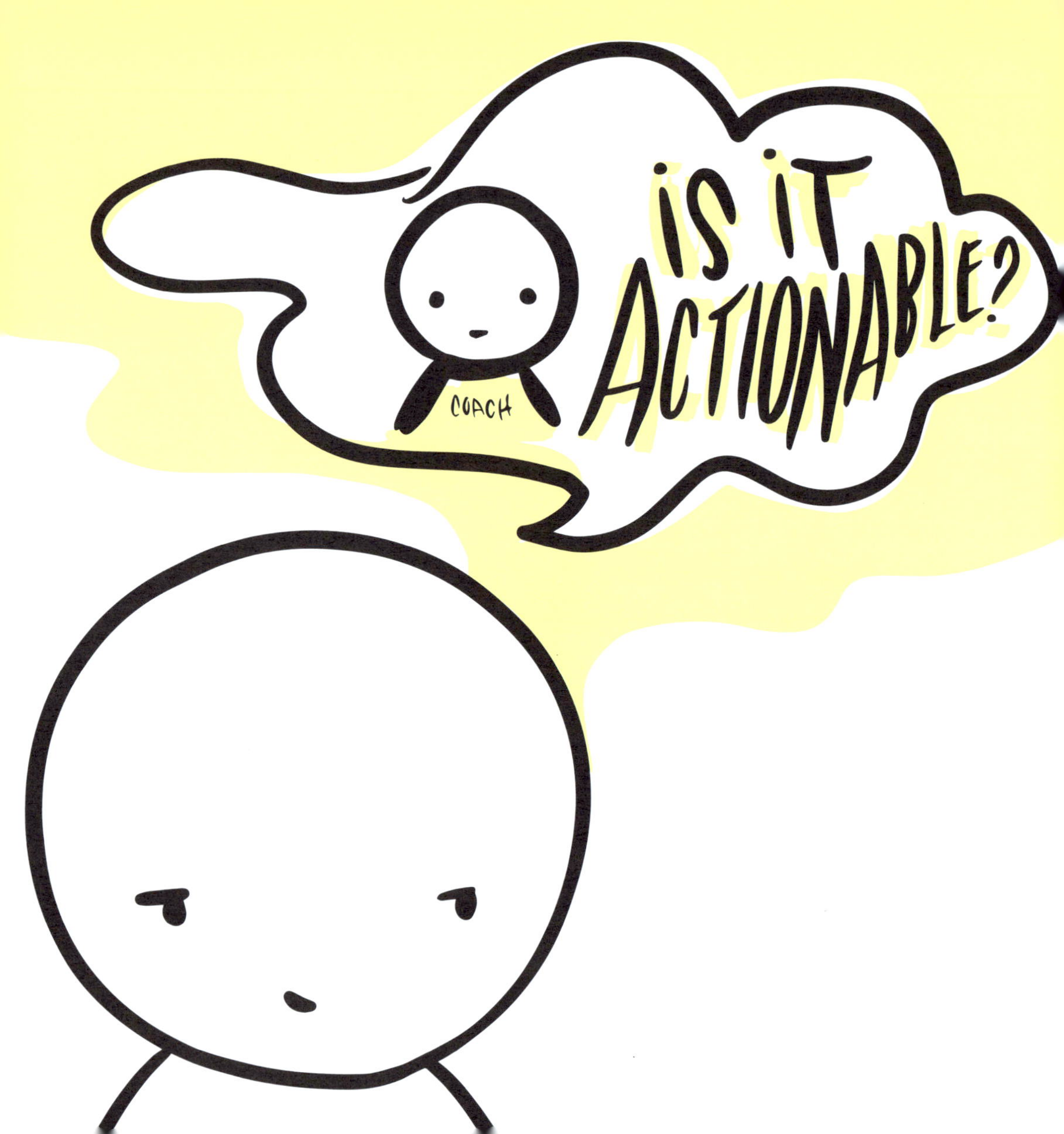
COACH
IS IT ACTIONABLE?

# The Heroic Question: Is It Actionable?

Is it *actionable*? A profound question in a simple package.

It's so powerful I call it the Heroic Question. A fork in the road. It has two answers: *Yes* or *No*.

How you answer sends you through *Yes Flow* toward your Action System. Or the *No Flow* toward your Storage System. Your answer shapes your life.

Continuing with our example:

- *I chipped my molar eating some popcorn and I need to get it fixed.*
- Is it actionable?
- *Yes*

Yes Flow, here we go...but before we do, let's take one deeper look at the Heroic Question.

# Deeper Questions

The Heroic Question—Is it actionable?—is an invitation to a conversation that's ultimately about something much bigger than a decision, a task, or a to-do.

**WHY** { am I saying YES / am I saying NO / am I saying YES when I want to say NO } **?**

You'll recognize parts of life that are in and out of your control.

The weather, the state of the economy, actions of a competitor, the actions of another person may be of concern but they are out of your control. The best you can do is respond.

Similar to the Serenity Prayer and many other wisdom teachings, the Heroic Question invites you to both engage and let go. Over time, and with practice, it will nurture and strengthen your inner wisdom.

Grant me the (Serenity) to accept the things I cannot change, the (COURAGE) to change the things I can, and the (WISDOM) to know the difference.

yes → flow

HERE WE GO

# Your Action System

Keep your word and build your confidence and trust.

Your Action System stores all the promises and agreements you make, big and small, until you complete them.

The format is simple; the value it delivers is profound.

- **Doing.** What's doing look like?
- **Done.** What's done look like?

Let's continue through the Yes Flow and build your Action System.

| **DOING** | **DONE** |
|---|---|
| **One Next Action** | **Project (Finish Line)** |
| *Doing Verb + Phrase* | *Phrase + Done Verb* |

# WHAT DOES DOING LOOK LIKE?

# What Does Doing Look Like?

One clear next action puts you in motion, creates momentum.

If this were the only thing for you to work on right now, what would you do?

- What's the very next action? (Doing verb + phrase)
- *Call the dentist to schedule an appointment.*

| **DOING** | **DONE** |
|---|---|
| **One Next Action** | **Project (Finish Line)** |
| *Doing Verb + Phrase* | *Phrase + Done Verb* |

*Call the dentist to schedule appointment.*

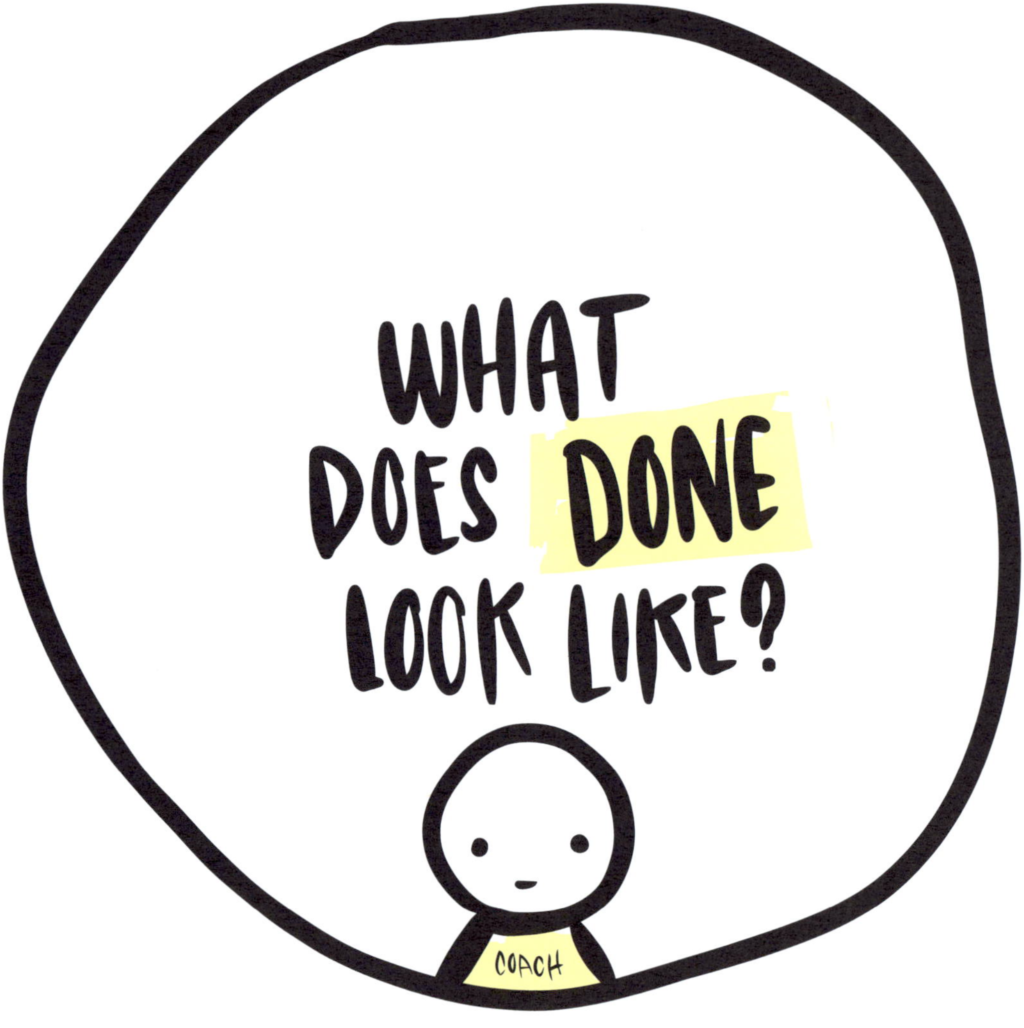
WHAT DOES DONE LOOK LIKE?
COACH

# What Does Done Look Like?

Done defines your finish line for a project. When you cross it, you win! Agreement kept, loop closed, trust and confidence rise.

- What's done look like? (phrase + done verb)
- *Chipped tooth repaired.*

Note: If you can close the loop with one action or one session, you can skip this step and write *single action* in this space (see next page for an example).

| **DOING** | **DONE** |
|---|---|
| **One Next Action** | **Project (Finish Line)** |
| *Doing Verb + Phrase* | *Phrase + Done Verb* |
| Call the dentist to schedule appointment. | chipped tooth repaired. |

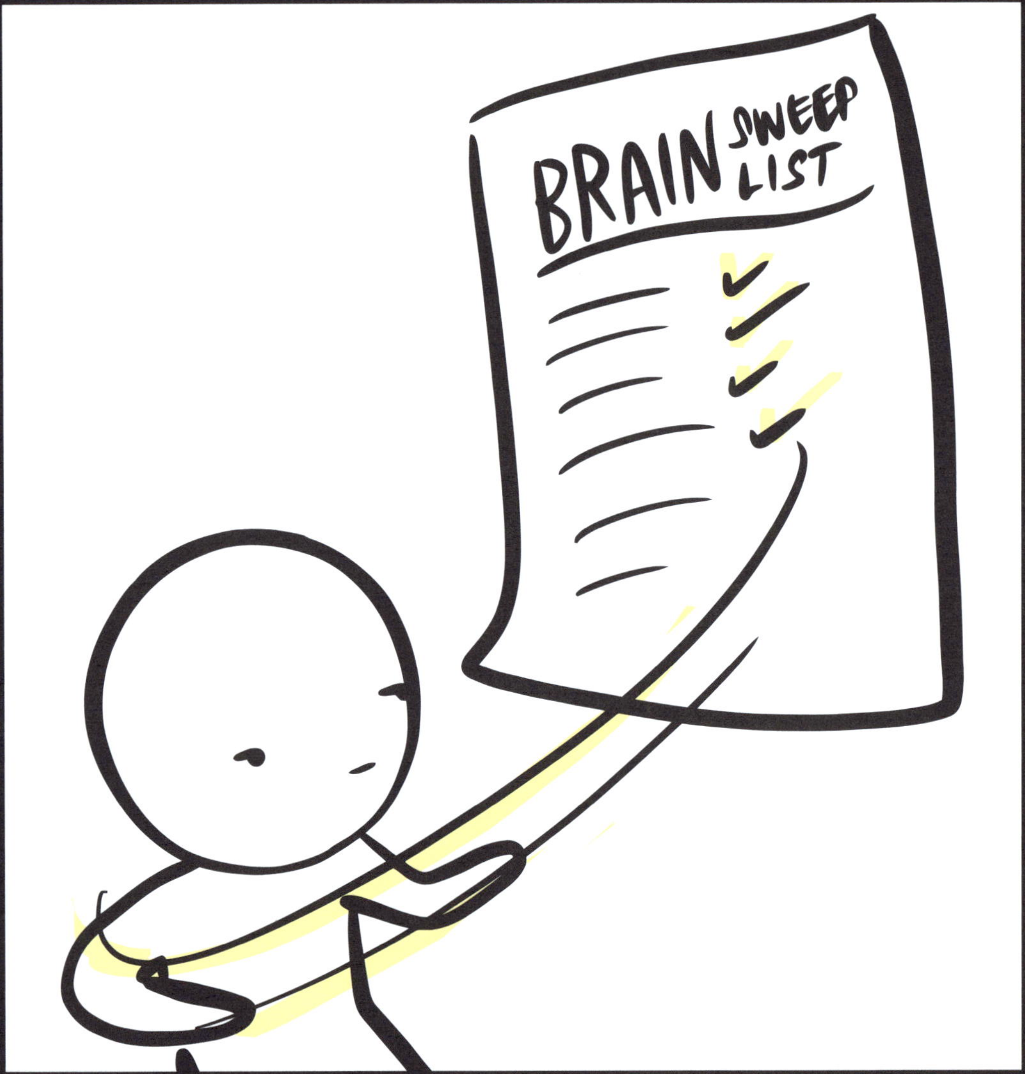
BRAIN SWEEP LIST

# Your Action System

| **DOING** | **DONE** |
|---|---|
| One Next Action | Project (Finish Line) |
| *Doing Verb + Phrase* | *Phrase + Done Verb* |
| Call the dentist to schedule appointment. | chipped tooth repaired. |
| Call Mom to catch up. | (single action) |
| Text Nick for mechanic name & phone number. | Engine situation resolved. |
| Waiting for Kristine (3/14) to send images. | Akimbo presentation delivered. |
| Block out Saturday to help Dad clean garage. | (single action) |
| Email basketball schedule & guidelines to parents. | youth basketball season completed. |

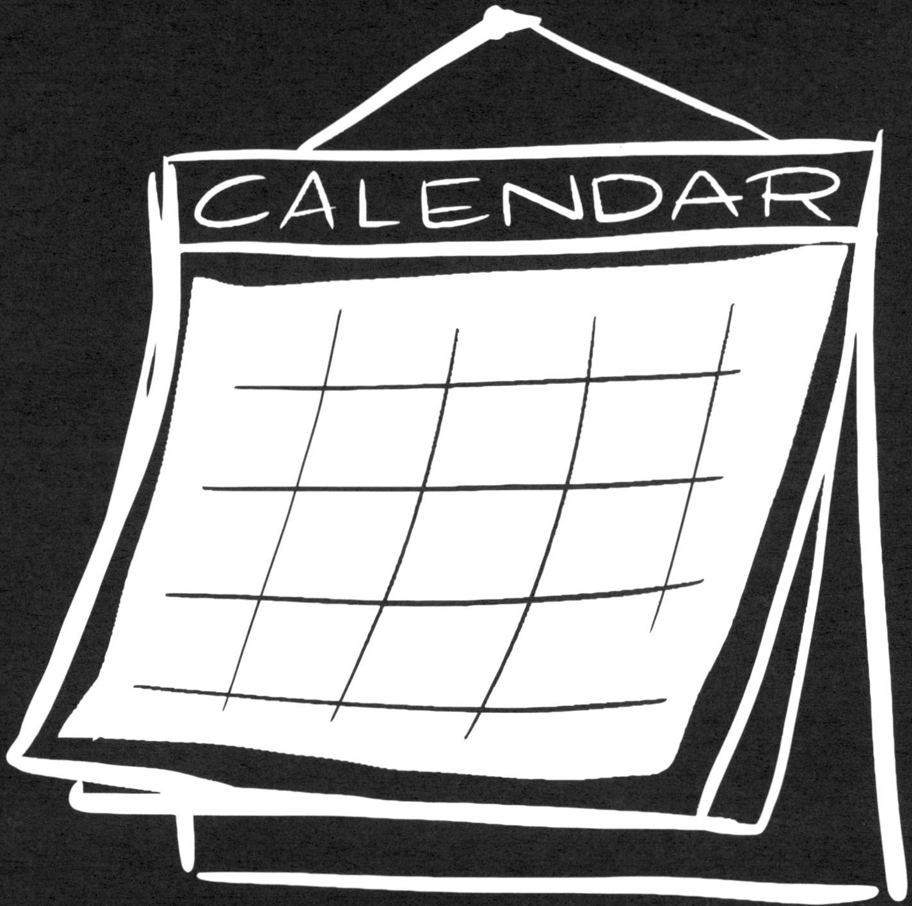
CALENDAR

# What Goes on Your Calendar?

Your calendar is one of your most important tools. Built strategically, checked daily, it keeps you on track.

Your calendar holds time-based actions. There are three major types:

1. Meetings
2. Appointments
3. Time-block spaces for focused work:
   - Space for project work
   - Space for practice work (e.g., gym time, writing time)
   - Space for actions that require focus and concentration

Each week it gets refreshed, your weekly fresh start.

Actions you defined that are not time-based remain on your Actions List, ready and waiting for you.

**PRESENT TENSE**

*Example:*
- Buy bread
- Call Mom
- Email team

- Buy...
- Call...
- Draft...
- Draw...
- Email...
- Fill...
- Fill out...

- Find...
- Gather...
- Google...
- Listen...
- Load...
- Call...
- Draft...

# DOING VERBS

- Draw...
- Email...
- Fill...
- Fill out...
- Find...
- Gather...
- Google...

- Listen...
- Load...
- Organize...
- Play...
- Print...
- Purge...
- Review...

- Schedule...
- Scout out....
- Search for...
- Take...
- Text...
- Waiting for...
- Watch...

**And there are many more.
You have the universe of action verbs
at your service.**

## PAST TENSE
*Example:*
- Car purchased.
- Mom's birthday celebrated.

## or PRESENT TENSE
*Example:*
- Purchase car.
- Celebrate Mom's birthday.

- …celebrated
- …clarified
- …completed
- …delivered
- …designed
- …established
- …finalized

# DONE VERBS

- …fixed
- …handled
- …implemented
- …installed
- …lived
- …optimized
- …organized
- …posted
- …published
- …reorganized
- …resolved
- …rolled out
- …set up
- …submitted
- …updated
- Look into…

**Like doing verbs, there are many more to choose from. Over time, you'll find your favorites.**

"THE QUESTION IS YOUR COACH."

# Recap

## Key Terms
- The Yes Flow
- Stuff
- Doing (Next action)
- Done (Project)
- Calendar

## Key Questions
- What is it?
- Heroic question: Is it actionable?
- What's doing look like? (doing verb + phrase)
- What's done look like? (phrase + done verb)

## Job it does
- Creates doing clarity (momentum).
- Defines done (the finish line).
- In a team or group setting, creates a common language.

## Key Ideas
- Store your agreements; keep your word; watch confidence and trust grow.

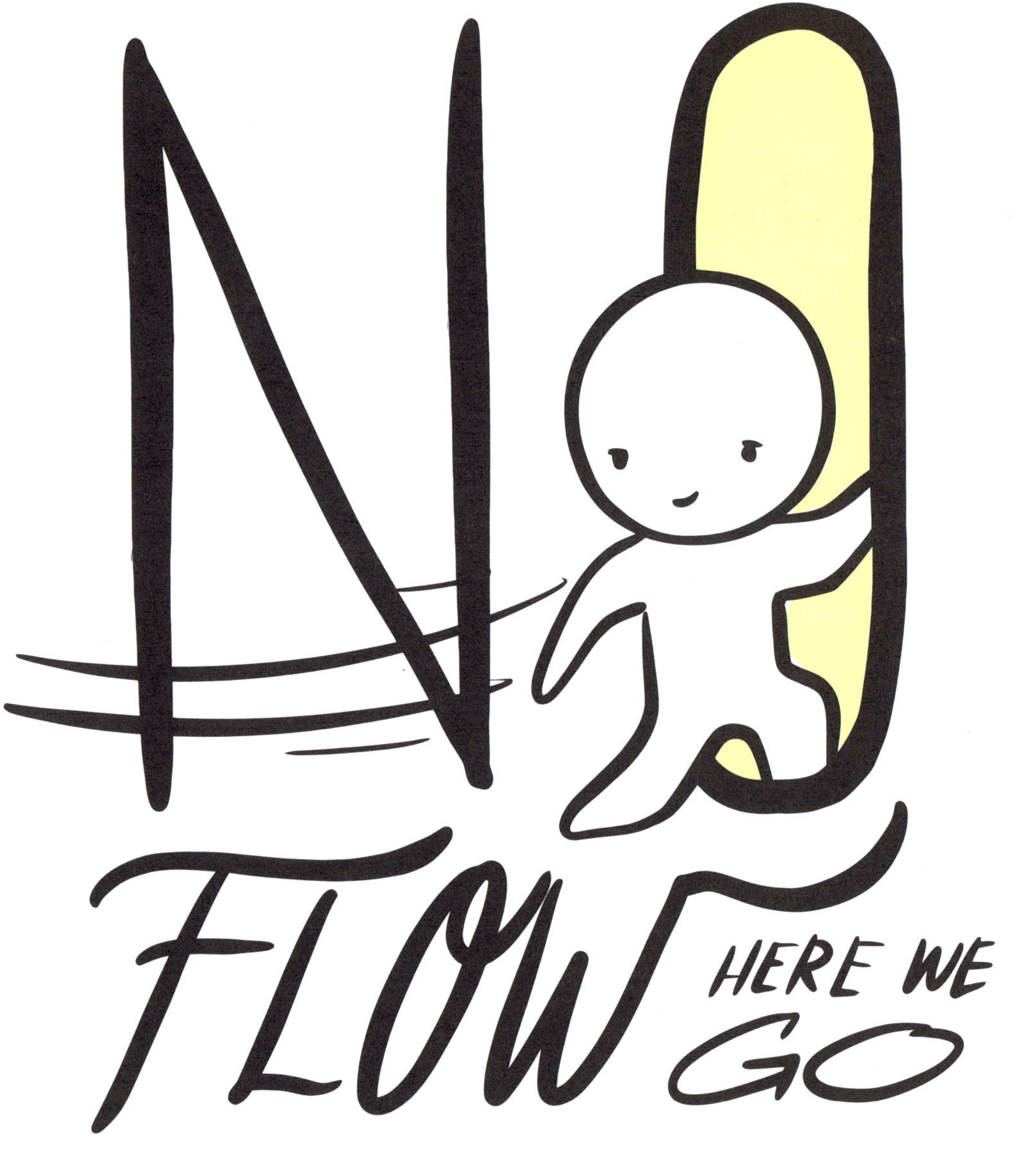
FLOW
HERE WE GO

# Your Storage System

Find what you need when you need it.

Have you ever thought, *Where did I put that?* or *Where do I put this?*

Your Storage System stores thoughts and items so you can find them when you need them, whether in digital systems or physical systems.

The blueprint is simple:

- A place for lists
- A place for reference materials and information

Trash, delete, or recycle items and information you don't need to store.

Let's continue through the No Flow path and build your simple, yet robust, Storage System.

# LISTs of LISTs

# Add It to a List?

The humble list is a phenomenal tool that stokes joy, creativity, and wonder.

Your imagination only limits the lists you create.

In your storage system, create a specific place for lists.

As a starting point I recommend creating a folder called *Lists of Lists*. Store a majority, if not all, of your lists here. You'll know exactly where to find your lists. They are all in your *List of Lists* folder.

Here's another tip, format the title of your list as follows: List-(Name of list). Examples: List-Books to read, List-Family clothing sizes, List-Quotes, List-Questions.

If stored digitally, you can easily find a list by searching for the word *list*.

Delight yourself and others with your wonderful lists.

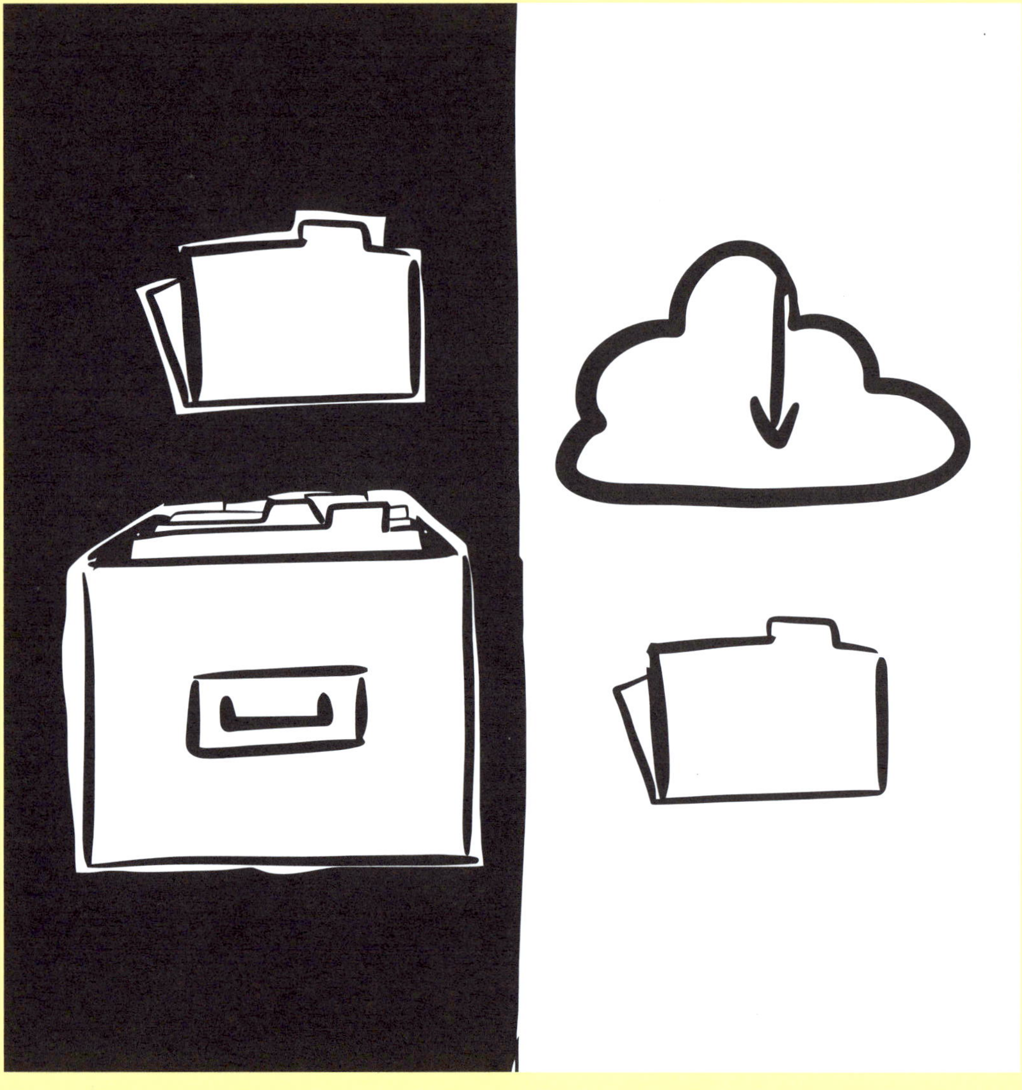

# Add to Reference?

Put a label on a box or folder and you now have a container for reference material. Put a matching item in the container. Presto! You're organized.

Think of reference storage as folders or boxes.

The most common ways to store reference information are physical storage and digital storage.

For physical storage, a filing cabinet with A-Z separators works magic. Second, boxes and containers with labels. In all my coaching, I find these two strategies solve most of the physical storage and retrieval needs.

For digital storage, there are a wide variety of options and specialty storage solutions. It's not uncommon for your digital storage to be spread across many systems. I strongly favor selecting a storage solution that is proven, will be around many years from now, and allows you to create hyperlinks to documents and folders. Hyperlinks help you cross-reference information so you can find it easily.

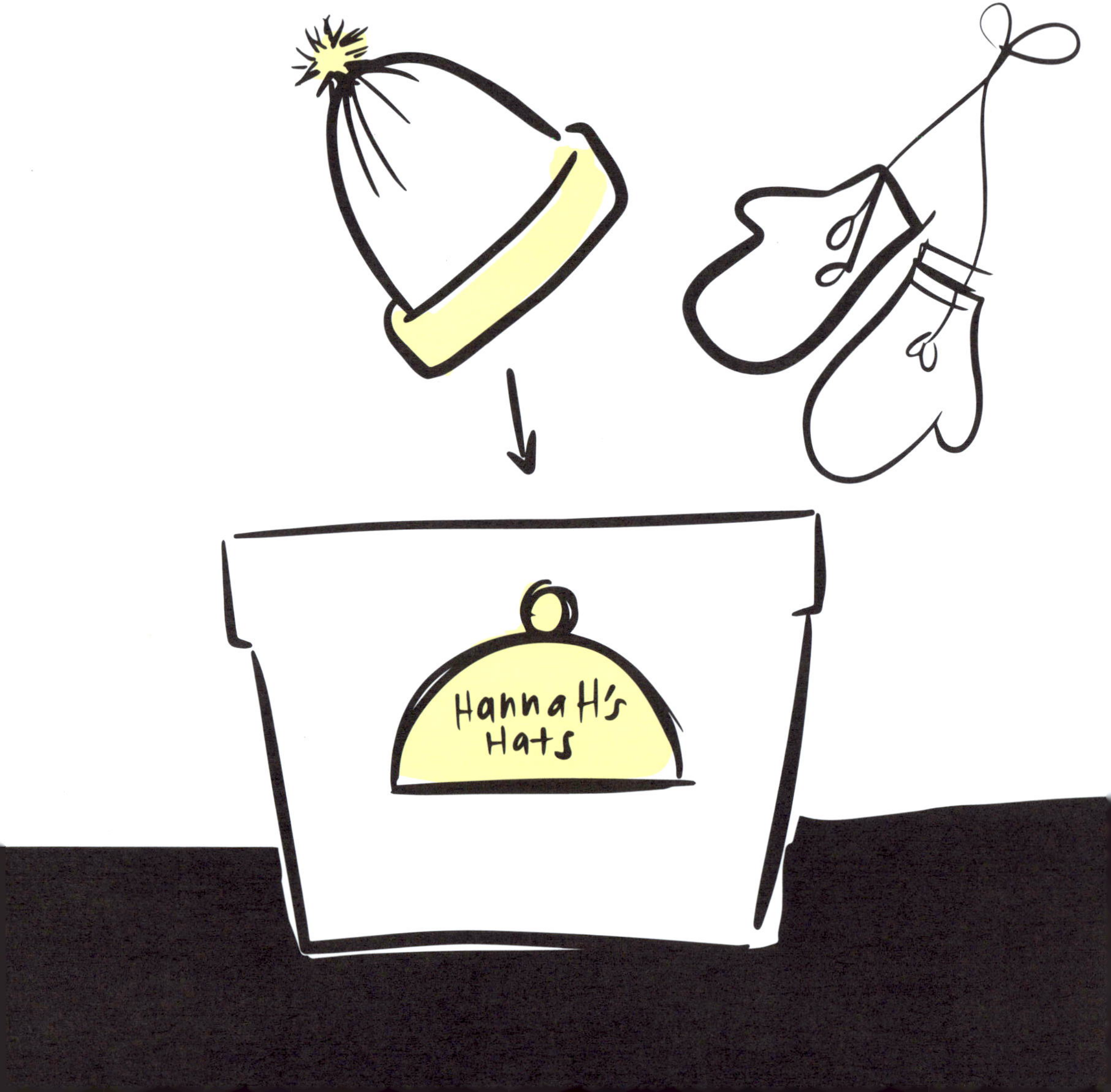
HannaH's
Hats

# Hats, Gloves, Scarfs

My son, Conrad, is four. My daughter, Hannah, is eight. We live in Vermont. It's winter. Our entryway from the garage to the kitchen is perpetually littered with hats, gloves, and scarfs.

Then one day, I have a bright idea! "Hey kiddos, let's play a game…"

We brought the mess from the entryway into the living room, creating one enormous pile of hats, gloves, and scarfs. I had the kids draw a picture of a hat, a glove, and a scarf and tape them to three buckets. Honestly, my son's pictures look like a blob, a blob, and a blob. Then I said, "See how fast you can get your hats, gloves, and scarfs into these buckets. I'll time you. Ready, set, go!"

A flurry of activity. Thirty-seven seconds later, the pile disappeared. Everything had a home.

In the business world we call this "Lean processing." At our home we call it the Hats, Gloves, Mittens game.

Put a label on a box; put the matching item in the box. You're organized. Simple.

# EXAMPLES of LISTS

- Affirmations
- Beers tasted
- Books to read
- Books to recommend
- Family clothing sizes and colors
- Gift ideas
- Ideas to incubate
- Local restaurants
- Next time in (place/city/country)
- Places to visit
- Quotes
- Questions
- Rec basketball team players
- Rec basketball team parents
- Scotch tasted
- Someday/Maybe
- Turns of phrase
- Wines tasted

**LIST
Books to read**

- *Drive*, Dan Pink
- *The Creative Habit*, Twyla Tharp
- *Decoded*, Jay-Z
- *The Overstory*, Richard Powers

ADD: *The Practice*, Seth Godin

# & REFERENCE

**Checklists**

- Basketball practice
- Babysitter
- Camp opening
- Camp closing
- Expense report process
- Keynote delivery
- Pet sitter
- Review, daily
- Review, weekly
- Review, quarterly
- Review, annual
- Tailgate
- Travel, business
- Travel, family
- Webinar presentation
- Workout routine

**Physical Reference**

- Birth certificate
- Books
- Death certificate
- Journals
- Passport
- Pictures (physical)
- Project reference material
- Safety deposit box
- Taxes (forms)
- Video (physical media)
- Wedding certificate

**Digital Reference**

- Project reference material
- Taxes (scanned)
- Pictures (cloud storage)
- Video (cloud storage)
- Web clippings

> "DELIGHT YOURSELF WITH YOUR WONDERFUL LISTS."

# Recap

## Key Terms
- The No Flow
- Lists
- Reference

## Key Questions
- Add to a list?
- Add to reference?

## Job it does
- Stores thoughts and items so you can find them when you need them.

## Key Ideas
- A trusted storage system helps you find what you need when you need it.

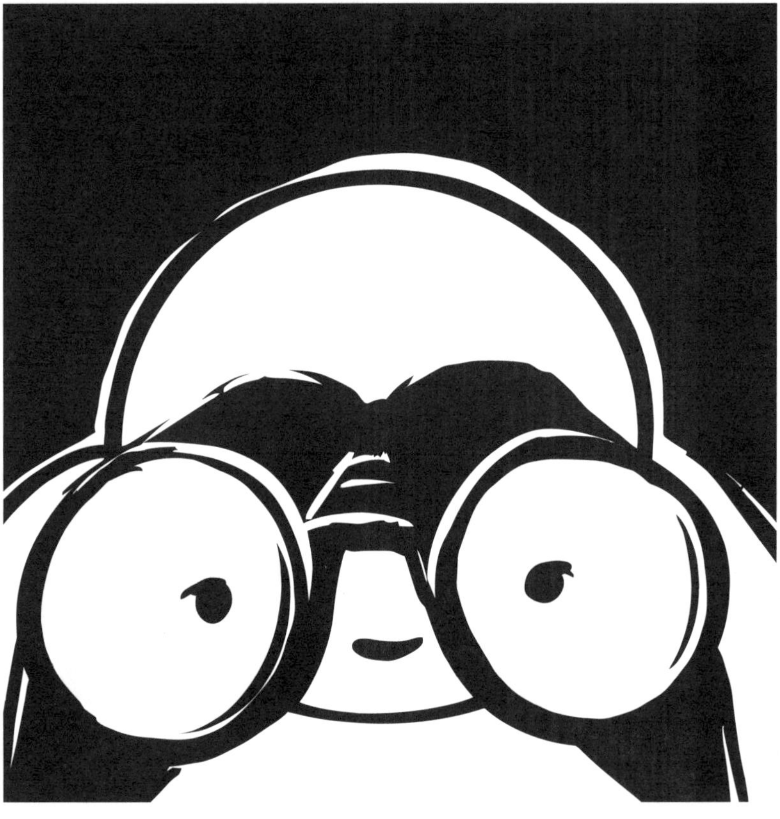

# Win #3 Review It

Build trust in your trusted system—stay at the top of your game.

With promises, agreements, and commitments in your Action System, *Review It* helps you keep them, renegotiate them, and complete them.

Once a week step back, move to a higher perspective, integrate recent information, and refresh your plan.

Review It involves three steps:

1. Review: Update your Action System.
2. Reflect: What am I grateful for? What did I learn?
3. Reset (fresh start): Update your priorities and refresh your plans.

See patterns, integrate current reality, and make progress on goals faster than ever, with much less effort.

Let's go through each step.

# REVIEW REF

## Core Review
- In your calendar, review previous week.

- In your calendar, review upcoming month.

- In your Action System, make sure each project has one next action.

## Advanced
- Review any relevant lists, checklists, or materials you want to see on a regular or temporary basis.

## Capture three things you're grateful for...

*1.*

*2.*

*3.*

# LECT

**Capture three things you learned...**

*1.*

*2.*

*3.*

# RESET

**Reset**

- Using your Action System, identify your top 3 projects for the coming week.

- Using your action system, identify your top 5 actions for the coming week.

- Create your fresh start: Update your calendar and time-block space for your priorities.

# Unabashedly be yourself!

# The X Factor

It's quarterly review time for each of the flock leaders at goodr.com (their name for managers), a fast-growing eyewear company in Southern California.

Besides their normal key performance indicators (KPIs), there is one keystone question that CEO (Chief Executive Octopus) Stephen Lease includes on every strategic review checklist: "Did you do your weekly review?"

Through personal experience, he knows it's the key to staying at the top of your game. It's his X factor. He values it so much, each employee gets time each week to do a review, and the importance gets reinforced during the quarterly review and it's baked into goodr OS, their cultural operating system.

Stephen wants his employees to work hard and play hard. You can't play hard and fully enjoy life if you're thinking about work all the time. He expects, sometimes demands, that people turn work off.

The review creates tremendous economic value for the company, but Stephen's striving for a grander vision: "We exist to give you permission to be unabashedly yourself… unless you're an asshole."

Review your system once a week; be your full self; live an epic life!

"A FRESH START EVERY WEEK."

# Recap

**Key Terms**
- Review
- Reflect
- Reset (fresh start)

**Key Questions**
- Does every project have a current next action?

**Job it does**
- Builds perspective.
- Cultivates gratitude.
- Creates continuous learning.
- Identifies priorities.
- Keeps system current and vital.
- Builds resilience.

**Key Ideas**
- Rise out of the detail, gain perspective, and create a fresh start every week.

To: the FUTURE YOU

♡: the PAST YOU

# Win #4
# Do It

Imagine how good you'd be at something if you'd completed one strategic action every day since your early days.

You capture your stuff (win!), transform it and store it in your Action System (win!), and review it (win!). Now is the moment to put your outstanding work into action.

Select one action—a love note from the *past you* to the *current you*. Put it in a work beat. One action, forward motion, doing. In-Do-Win!

Bust through resistance and procrastination; feel momentum building.

Imagine how good you'll feel in one week, one month, one decade as you complete one strategic action every day and feel the joy of small wins that feed your soul.

# SPACE TO...

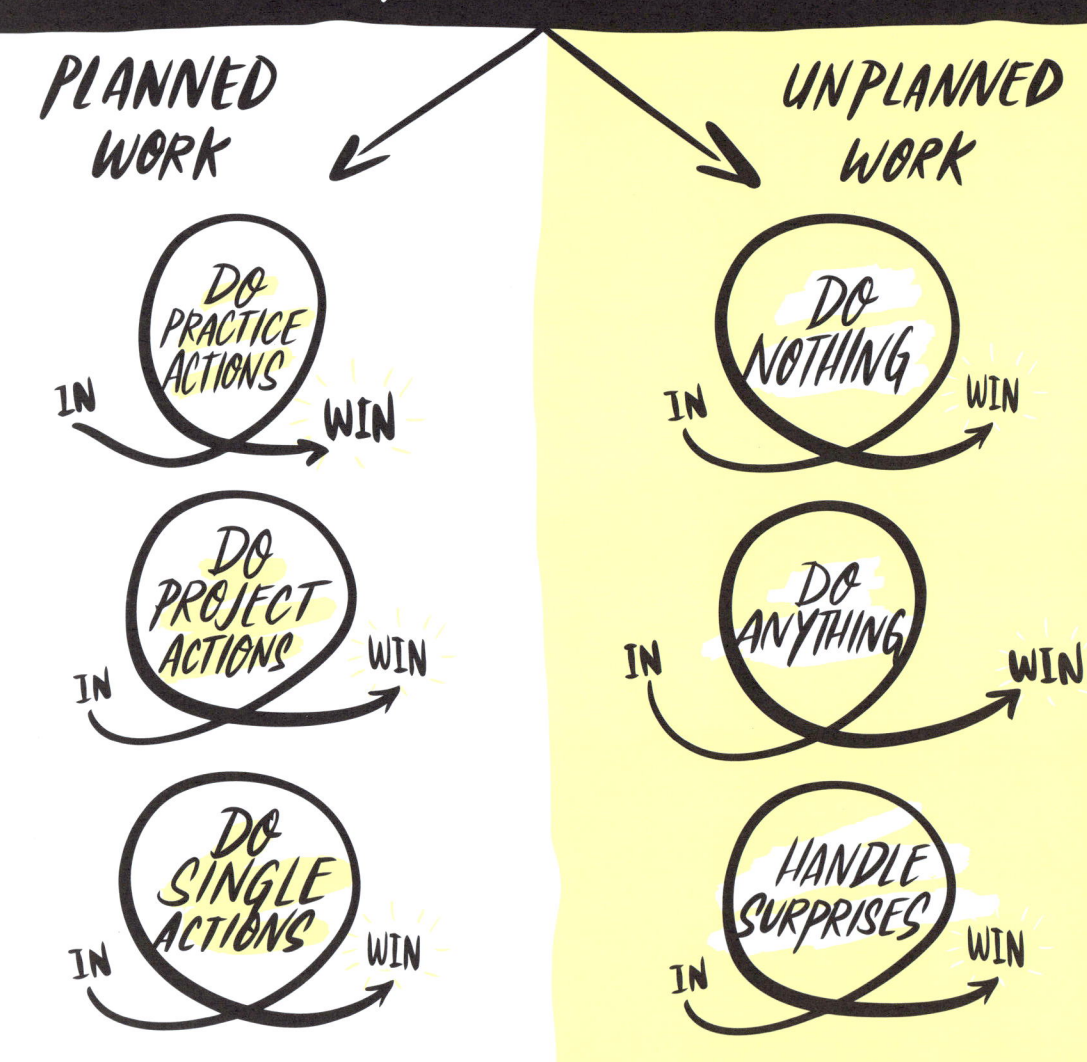

## PLANNED WORK

- DO PRACTICE ACTIONS — IN → WIN
- DO PROJECT ACTIONS — IN → WIN
- DO SINGLE ACTIONS — IN → WIN

## UNPLANNED WORK

- DO NOTHING — IN → WIN
- DO ANYTHING — IN → WIN
- HANDLE SURPRISES — IN → WIN

# Types of Doing

Moment to moment, you choose between two categories of doing:

- Do planned work.
- Do unplanned work.

When you do planned work, you make progress on the agreements and promises you made with yourself and others. Building trust.

Your Action System holds your planned work. It helps you handle unexpected surprises and step away from your work so you can do unplanned work with a sense of joy and freedom and release feelings of guilt, anxiety, and overwhelm.

Things like long walks, vacation, playing with your child, recreation, and daydreaming.

"SELECT ONE ACTION... PUT IT IN A WORK BEAT... IN-DO-WIN!"

# Recap

## Key Terms
- Doing (one action)
- Work beat (In-Do-Win)
- Planned work
- Unplanned work

## Key Questions
- What is the optimal action? (Which includes strategically doing nothing.)

## Job it does
- Doing planned work builds trust.
- Doing one action creates momentum.
- Planned work creates space for unplanned work.

## Key Ideas
- Imagine how good you'll feel in one week, one month, one decade as you complete one strategic action every day.

# The Project Clarity Map

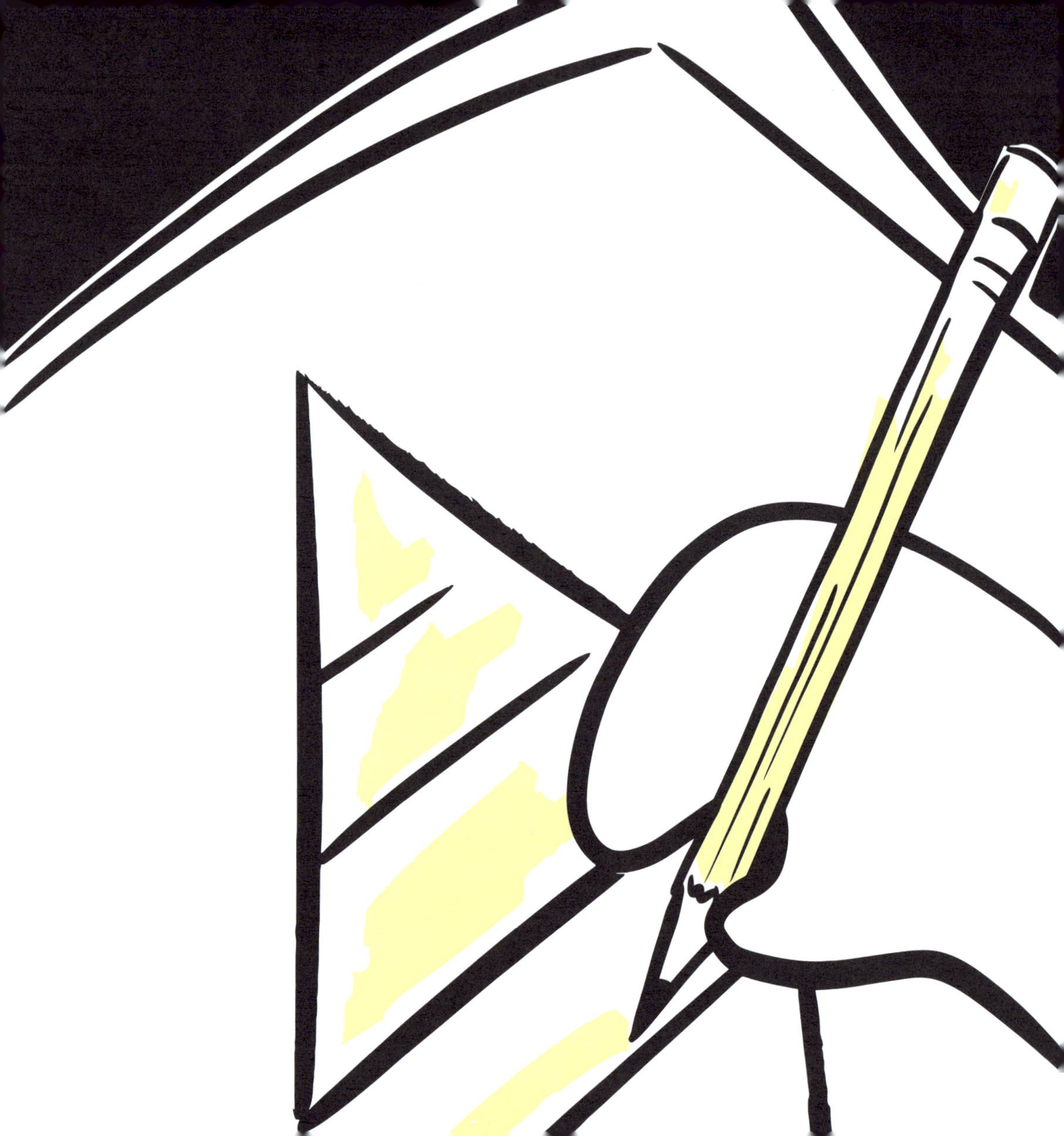

# Plan Like a Pro

Complete projects with purpose and confidence, and achieve outstanding results—with much less effort and hassle.

The Project Clarity Map is like DNA, a primary form with infinite uses.

It's a game changer. Harness your inspiration and vision, release creativity, and create clarity with ease.

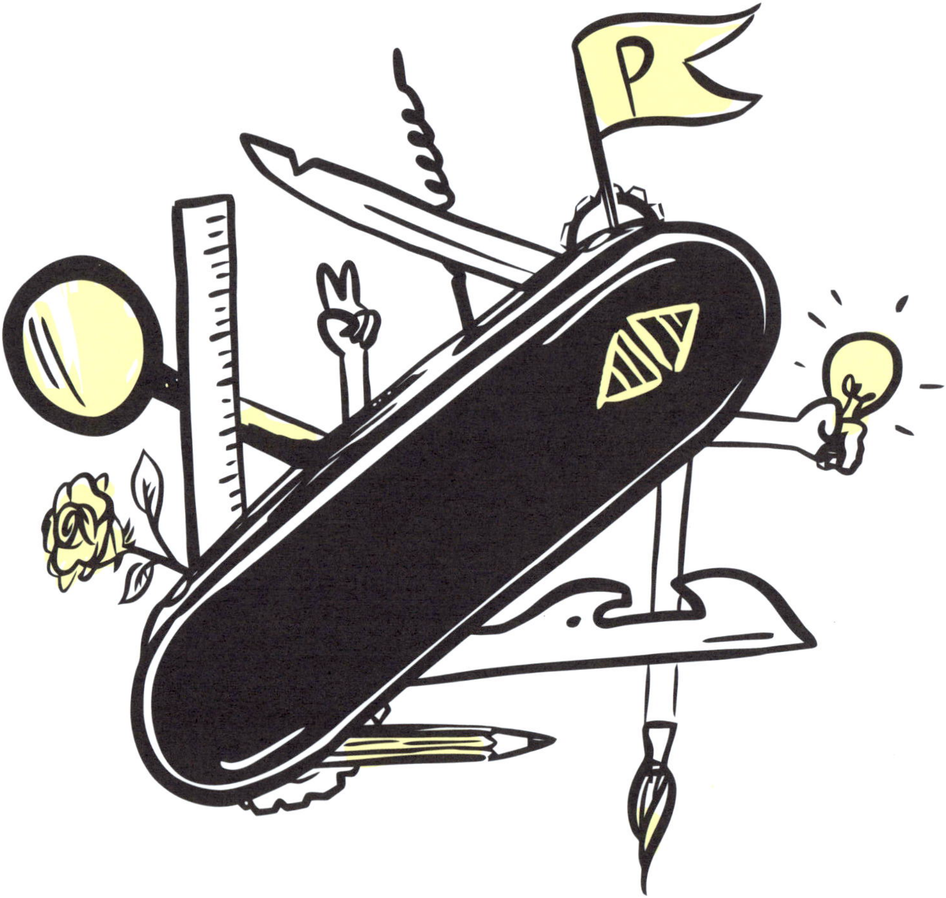
P

# Project Clarity Map

The Project Clarity Map is the Swiss Army knife of productivity tools, and a real career enhancer.

In a work context, I've used it to:

- help teams and companies create a consistent approach for launching and tracking projects.
- help leaders plan speeches and write high-stakes emails.
- plan large company meetings and retreats.
- create strategic account plans to delight customers and increase sales.
- help executives plan a company-wide restructuring.
- guide a leader through a difficult conversation involving a higher level executive.
- help a leader create a plan to take vacation time—guilt free.

In a personal context, I've used it to:

- help people find new jobs, plan weddings, plan care for an elderly parent.
- help students write essays for college applications.
- create practice plans for a high school volleyball coach. (PS: They won the state championship!)

It's a must-have tool for your leadership toolbox.

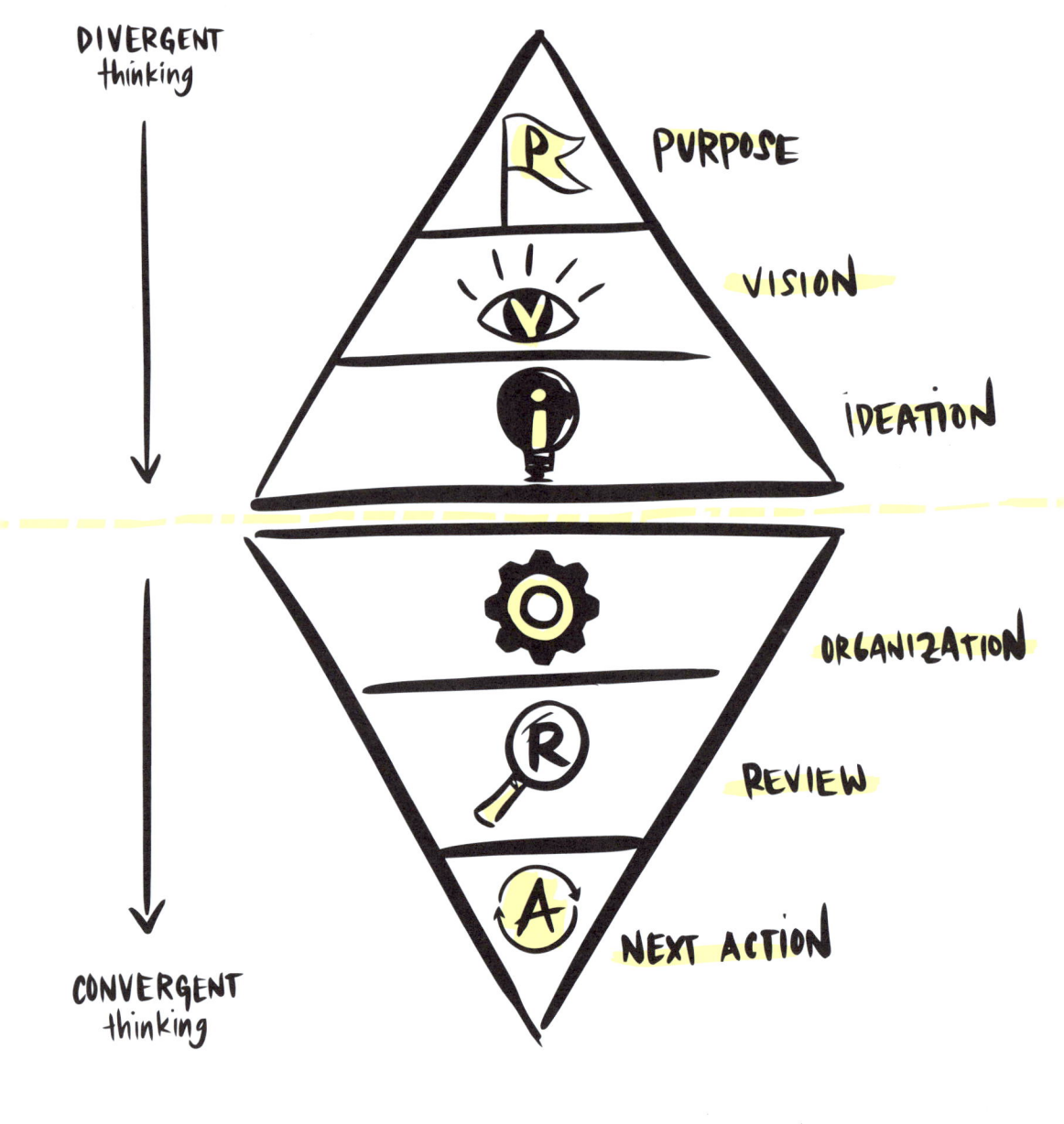

**DIVERGENT thinking**

- PURPOSE
- VISION
- IDEATION
- ORGANIZATION
- REVIEW
- NEXT ACTION

**CONVERGENT thinking**

# The Two Sides of Clear Thinking

The Project Clarity Map harnesses the power of divergent and convergent thinking.

It has a unique diamond shape, and two distinctive parts:

1. Divergent thinking: Define the project's purpose, capture the vision of success, and make space to generate ideas.
2. Convergent thinking: Organize ideas into a plan, review your plan against the stated purpose and vision of success, and define one next action that will move the plan forward.

Let's walk through the steps together and put this important tool in your leadership toolbox. Select a project that's important to you.

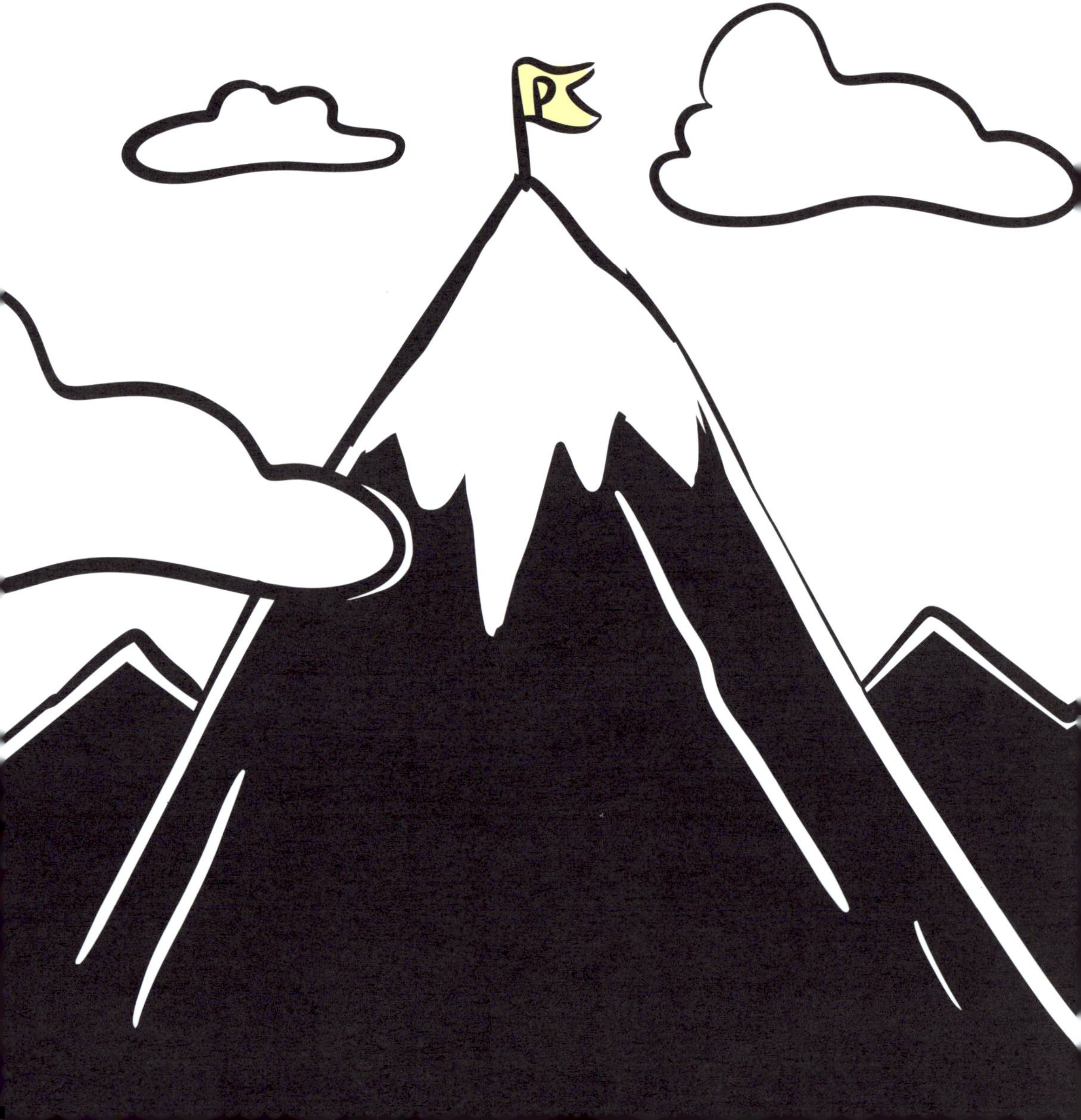
P

# Purpose

First step, define the project's purpose. The project name clarifies the endpoint/goal. The project's purpose defines why you want to go on this journey. Writing your purpose statement has a powerful clarifying effect.

Purpose statements are succinct. They have two common forms:

1. To *contribution*
2. To *contribution* so that *impact*

Examples:
- Project: *Mid-year business review completed*
    - Purpose: *To increase business predictability across all functions so that we learn, we grow the business, and we help employees grow in their careers.*
- Project: *Zen space created on 4th floor*
    - Purpose: *To create a silent space for employees*
- Project: *Look into new job opportunities*
    - Purpose: *To grow my career so I can gain experience, evolve as a professional, and increase my earning potential.*

Purpose is your project's North Star.

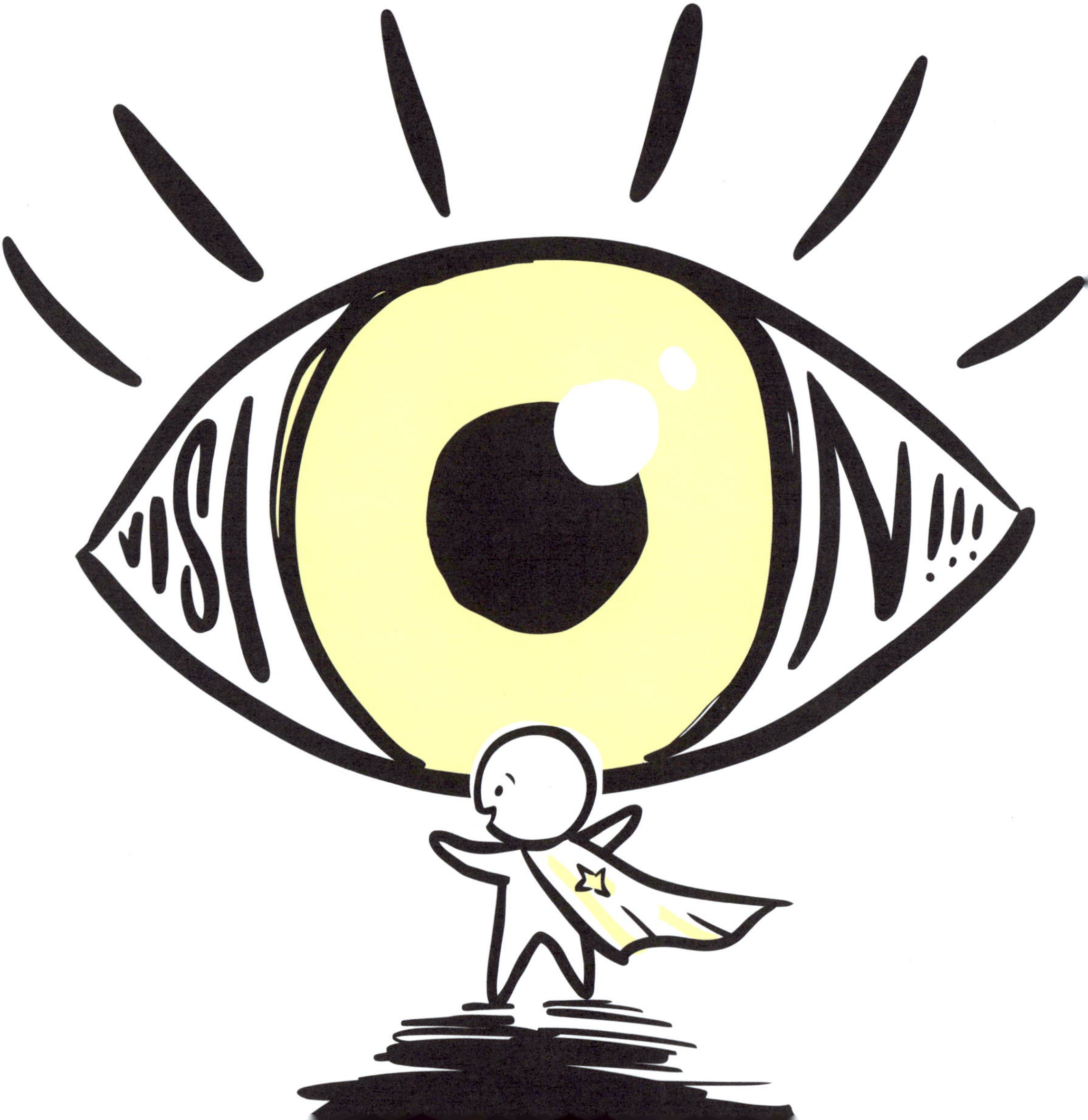
VISION!!!

# Vision

Second step, what's your vision of wild success for the project?

Imagine the project is over. It's a success—a wild success! You caused such a buzz a reporter hears about the project and wants to do a feature article.

- What's the headline?
- Who's the customer?
- What problem did you solve?
- What quotes did the reporter capture from your customers, stakeholders, and you?

Your answers can range from a couple bullet points to a couple paragraphs to a full mock-up of a feature article, pictures and all. Your brain loves rich imagery.

We are all about small wins that are fun and increase your success. A well-defined purpose and vision puts you on the same page so you can get your project done on time with the least amount of effort.

With your well-defined vision, you're ready for the next step.

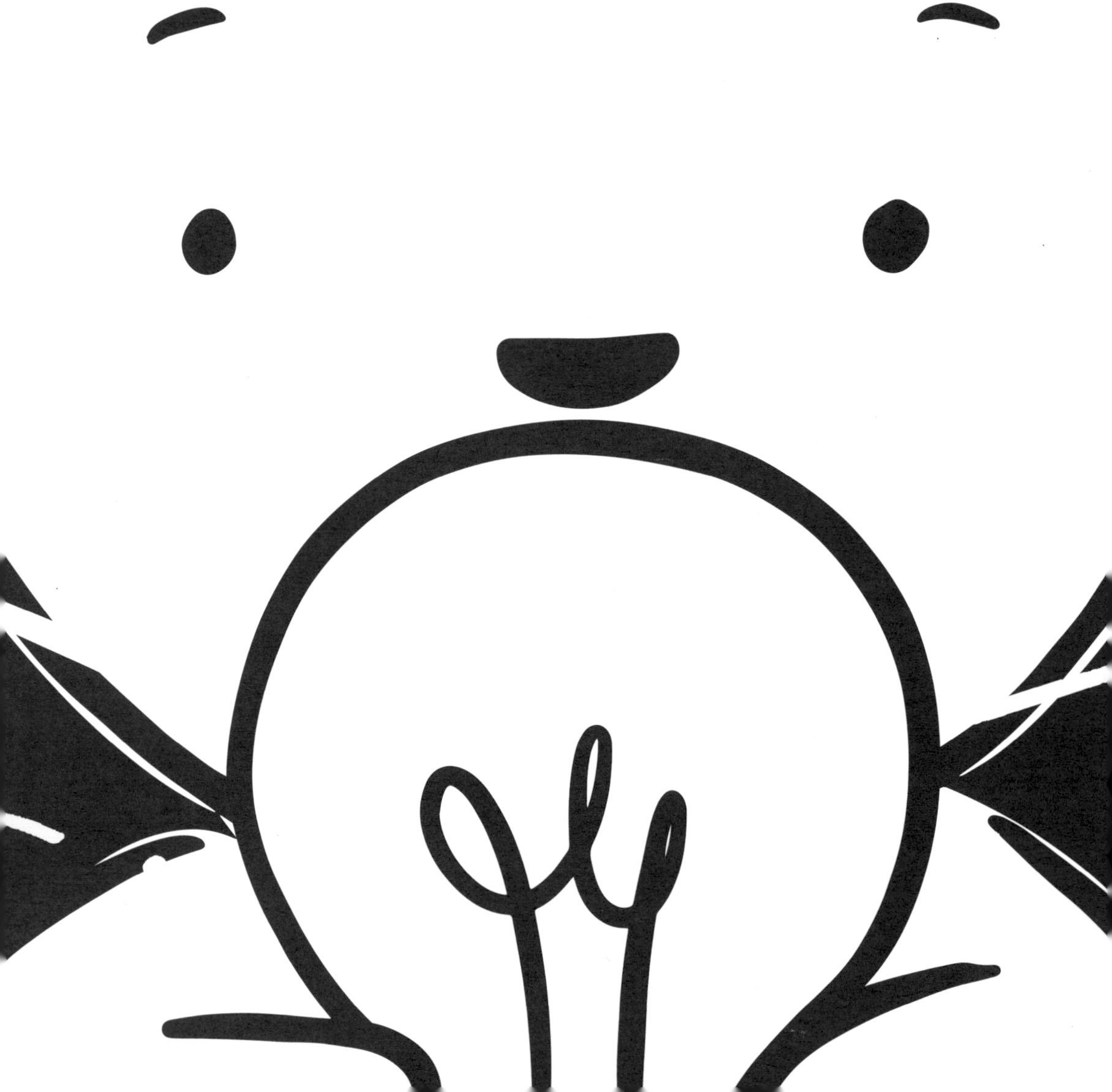

# Ideation

Third step, with your purpose and vision set, rev up your imagination engine.

Ideation is about generating as many ideas as you can so you can turn your purpose and vision into reality.

- Get ideas out of your head as quickly as you can. Go for quantity over quality.
- Great ideas emerge from your piles of good, not-so-good, and bizarre ideas. Ideation is all about opening your creative flow.
- Use ideation tools and techniques that best fit your situation. Pen and paper, sticky notes, index cards, mind maps, group collaboration software—there are a lot of options to choose from.

But wait, if you spend too much time generating ideas, things get a little crazy and unproductive. When you notice this tension, it's a signal you've reached the outer boundary of divergent thinking.

Stop generating; let's organize your ideas.

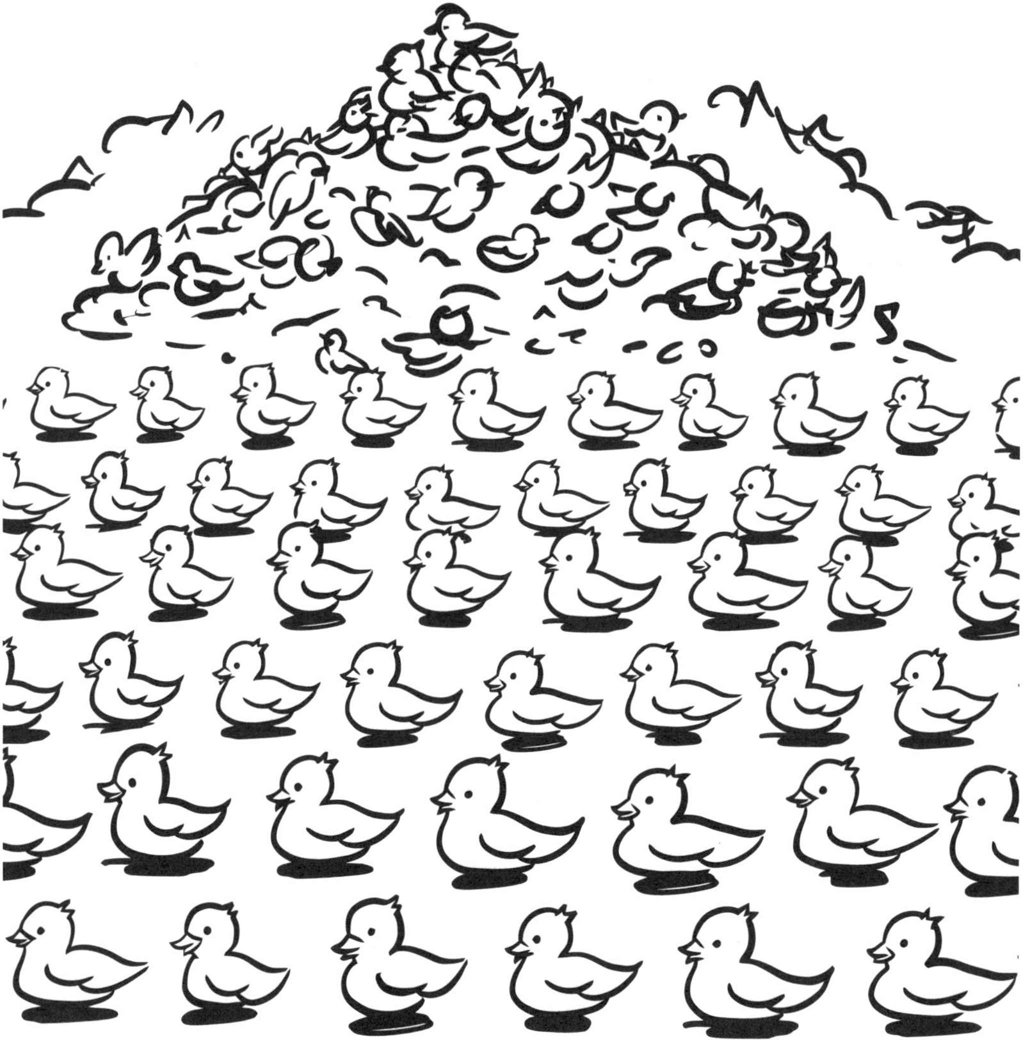

# Organization

Fourth step, plan like a pro, get your ducks in a row, and watch your confidence grow. With a host of ideas to draw from, you're set up for success. It's time to organize.

Projects range from simple to complex. Here are some of the most common formats for organizing projects, sorted from lower to higher complexity.

- ***Project name and next action***: You can manage many of your projects by simply defining the project name and having a current next action. For example, Project: *Passport renewed*, Next Action: *Fill out renewal form.* Seeing your project name and your next action creates momentum.
- ***List, outlines, mind maps***: Some projects require more thinking and planning. In this situation, use a list, outline, or mind map to organize your plan. For example, when planning a wedding or large celebration, you might organize your actions into an outline grouped by categories, such as Venue, Food, Music, Guest List. That's enough to keep you on track.
- ***Templates, project workflows, project planning software***: Some of your projects may belong to a professional domain with complex workflows and more sophisticated tools you will use. For example, product development or construction planning.

Select the best format, organize your ideas, relax, and stay on track.

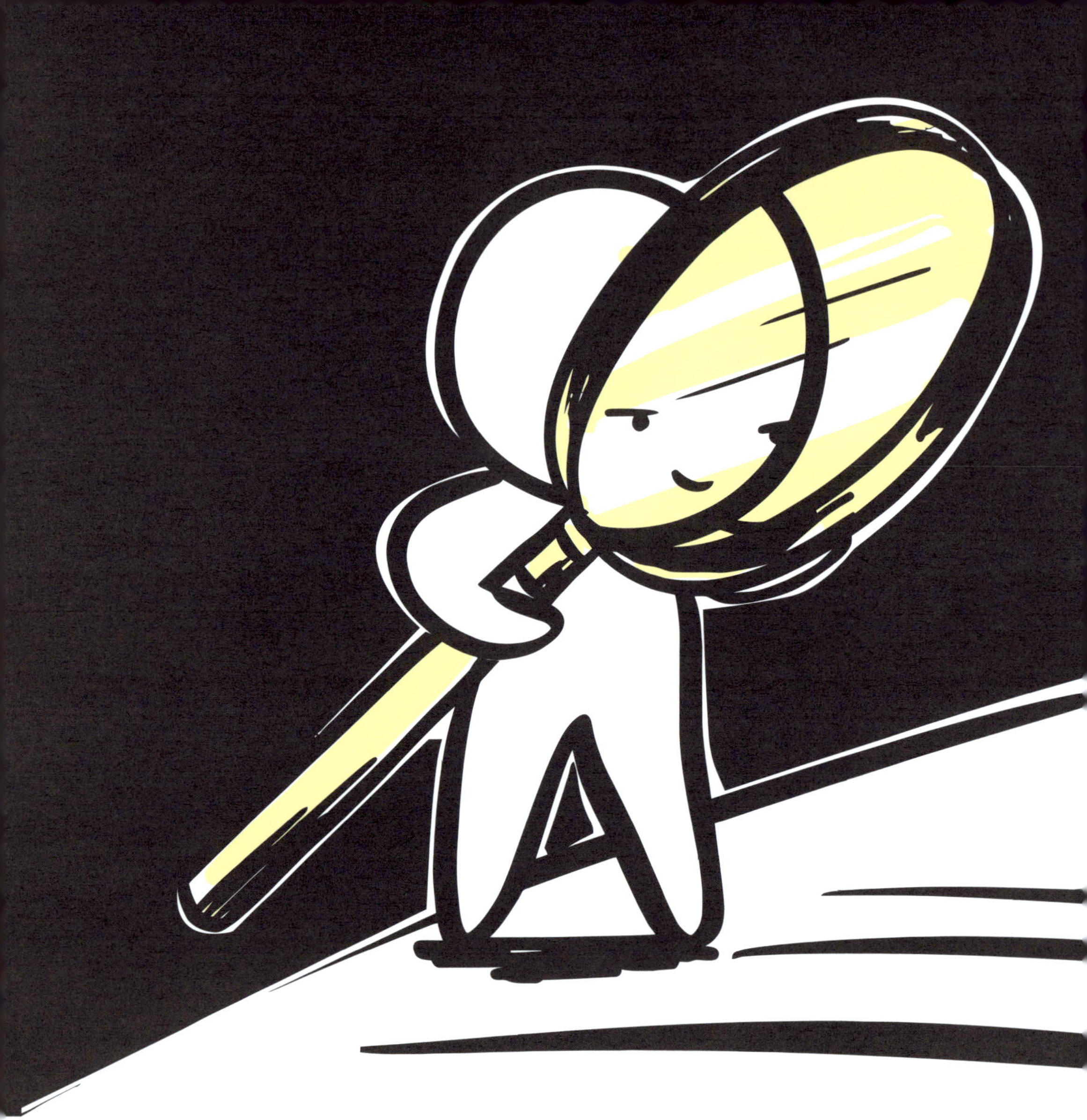

# Review

Fifth step, delight yourself, your coworkers, and your customers. Avoid the agony of ambiguity.

Time to review your plan and ask a critical question: Will the plan accomplish your purpose and get you to your vision of success?

Get to yes; increase your success.

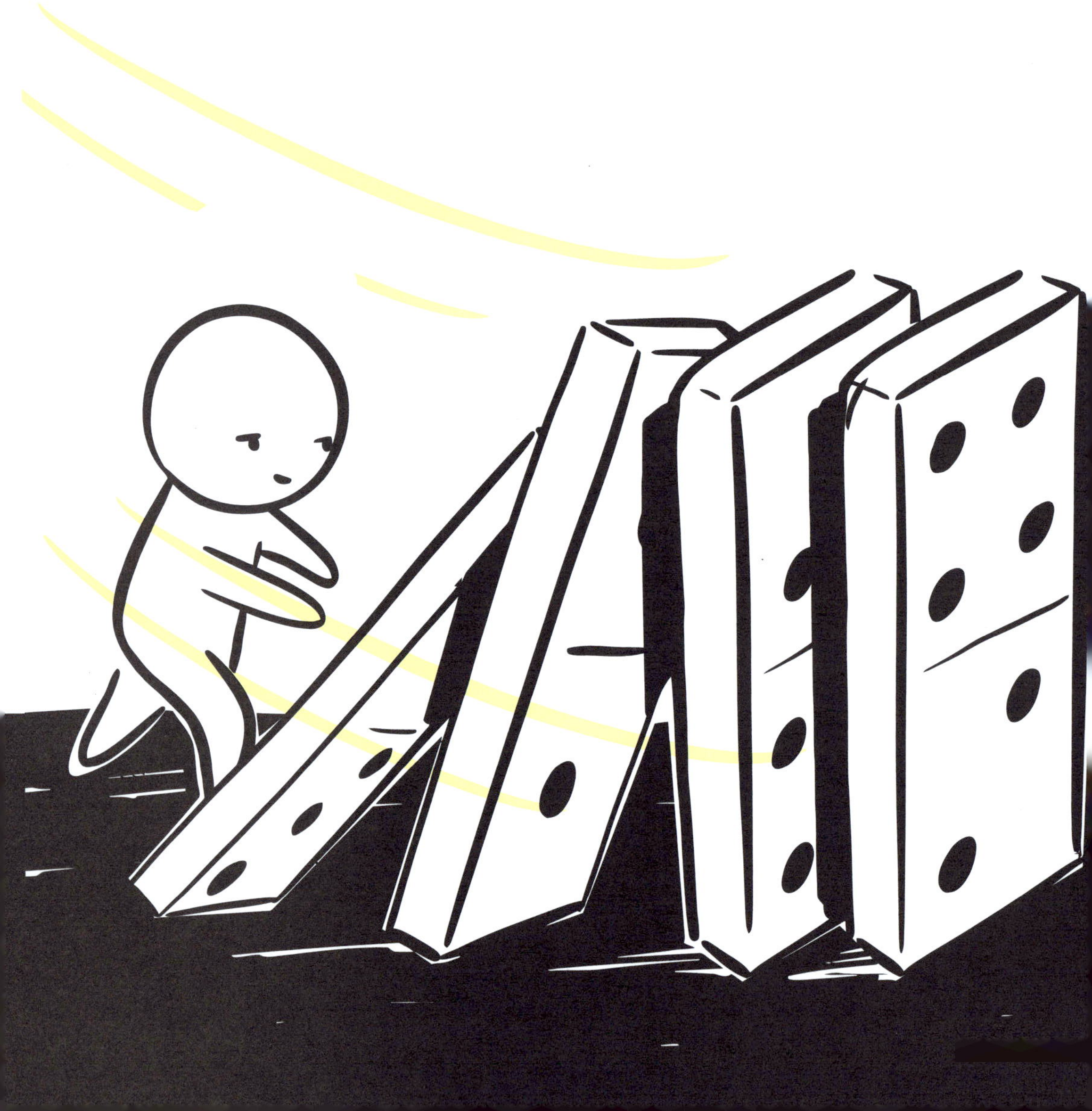

# One Next Action

Sixth and last step, projects share one thing in common: they move forward when somebody takes action.

- What's the next action?
- Who owns it?

Congratulations! With those questions, you create momentum. Turn ideas into action.

Use the Project Clarity Map to plan like a pro, watch your effectiveness improve, and feel your confidence grow.

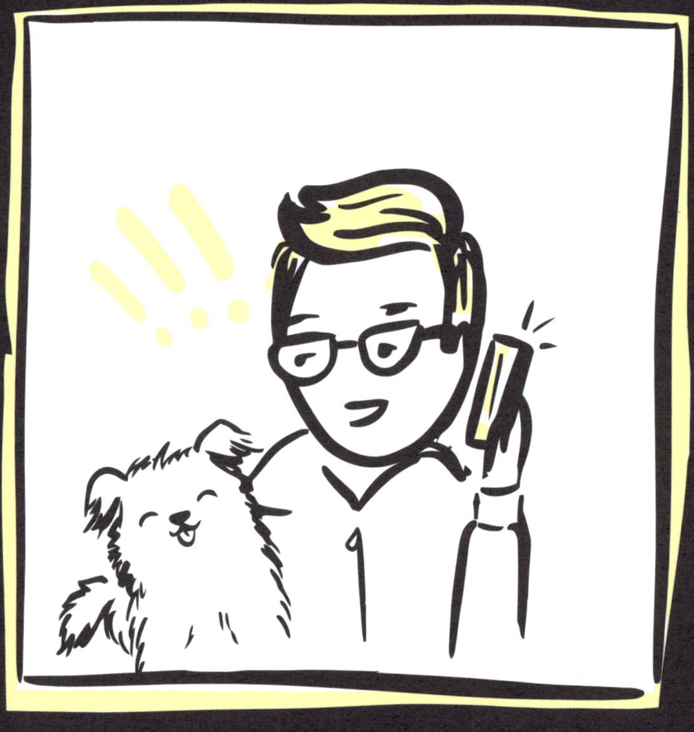

# Goodbye Problems

Friday arrives and I sign in. Adam's video flickers to life; he's in a maroon zip-up hoodie, three days of stubble, and his dog Maddie is on his lap licking his face. I'm greeted with a long sigh, a blank stare, and "Hey."

"I'm meeting with Sofia in two days in L.A. We've got some problems I need to discuss. I don't like conflict…I'm not really well equipped for this…not really skilled in having these conversations… they create anxiety…I'm not really sure how to approach these things…"

"You know the Project Clarity Map we used on your project last week? The same steps apply here. Problems are simply projects."

"Let's start at the top; let's frame this as a project. What's the project name? What's the purpose of the meeting with Sofia? Your vision of success?" His eyes light up, thoughts pour out, and words fly across the screen.

Three days later Adam calls. "Thank you. I had a great meeting with Sofia. I shared the purpose of the meeting, my vision of success, and asked for hers. It went really well. I felt confident in the conversation, and best of all we landed in a great place."

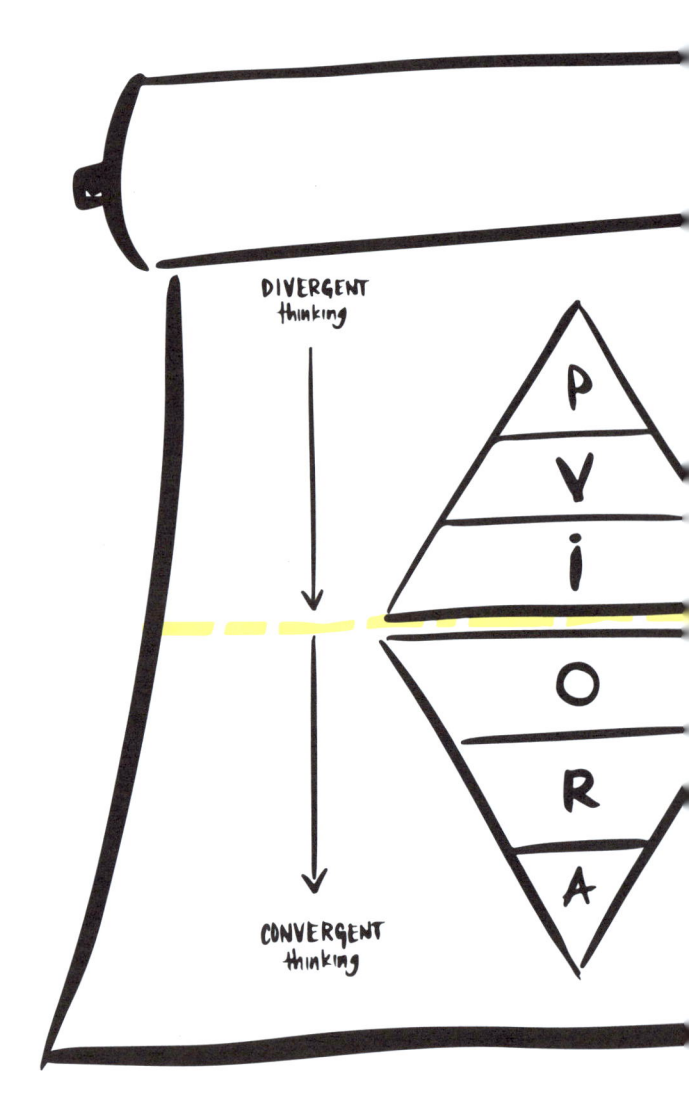

# YOUR
## PROJECT
### CLARITY
#### MAP

DIVERGENT
thinking

CONVERGENT
thinking

P
V
I
O
R
A

→ PURPOSE ~~~   VISION ~~~
                        ~~~
                        ~~~.

IDEATION

ORGANIZATION

REVIEW

NEXT ACTION ~~~

"Harness your inspiration and vision, release creativity, and create clarity with ease."

# Recap

## Key Terms
- Project name
- Divergent thinking: Purpose, Vision, Ideation
- Convergent thinking: Organization, Review, Action

## Key Questions
- What's the purpose of the project?
- What's your vision of wild success?
- What ideas do you have?
- How can they be organized?
- What's the next action to move the project forward (*Doing verb + phrase*)?

## Job it does
- Complete projects with purpose, confidence—with much less effort and hassle.

## Key Ideas
- The Project Clarity Map is like DNA, a primary form with infinite uses. Learn the form, increase your effectiveness, and delight your customers.

# The Role Clarity Map

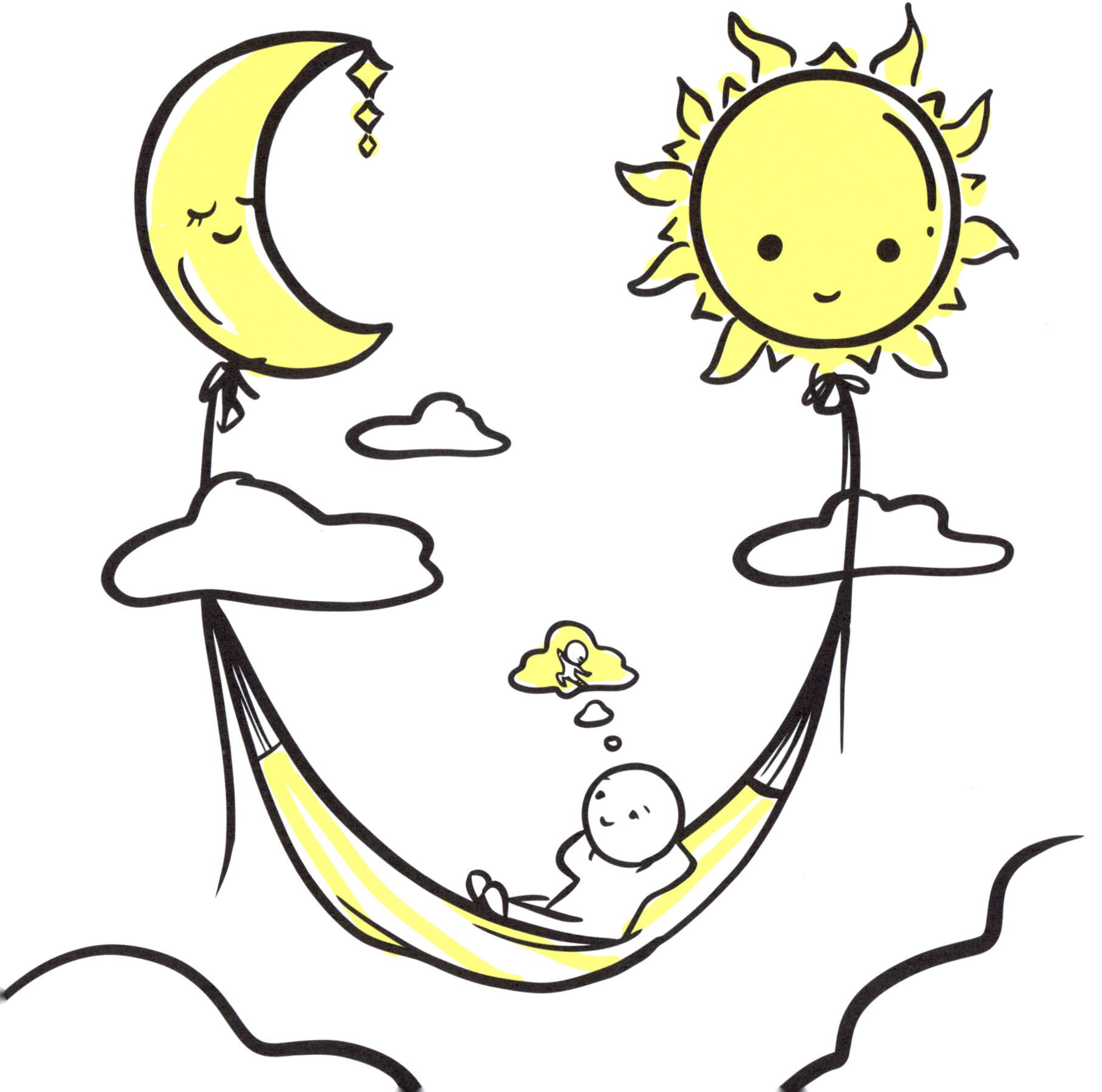

# The Role of Roles

Energize your dreams, spark your imagination, and create clarity with roles.

Name your roles, define your intentions, and put inspiration in your actions.

Let's meet a few everyday heroes like us and explore the role of roles.

# HEROES LIKE US

## Conrad

*A year ago Conrad was in high school, living at home, skateboarding with his friends.*

*Today he is a full-time college student, lives on his own, has a girlfriend, and works two jobs.*

*Adjusting to his first taste of freedom.*

## Hannah

*A recent college graduate who, after a couple temporary jobs and a brief stay at home, landed her first "real" job.*

*She signed a lease for her first apartment with a new roommate.*

*Excited to start her next phase of life.*

## Keri

*Co-founded a fast-growing business in her twenties, while pursuing an acting career. The last five years were a blur.*

*She's a busy artist and entrepreneur, juggling responsibilities.*

*The business side is squeezing out her art aspirations. She's contemplating what's next for her.*

## Jeff

*Twenty years into his career, a vice president for a global outdoor brand.*

*He's a husband, father of three spanning middle school, high school, and college. His mother recently died, his father has eldercare needs—and he's a high school volleyball coach striving for another state championship.*

*A doer, creator, global traveler who's juggling many responsibilities. Life is full.*

## Gina

*Early in her career, Gina was a sports medicine doctor.*

*Today she's a stay-at-home mom of two teen boys, a wife, a homeschooling parent and teacher.*

*With her boys on the cusp of leaving home, she's exploring her next move.*

## Maggie

*A single mom whose only son recently graduated from college and moved across the country to start his career.*

*Her father recently died. She's handling his estate while downsizing her home, moving to a new state, and reviving her consulting business.*

*She's closing chapters of life and opening new ones.*

**WHY**

**ROLE**

**HOW + WHAT**

# The Role Clarity Map

The Role Clarity Map is a simple yet powerful method for visualizing your roles.

At the core is a set of brief notes to yourself that describe each role, organized around the why and how/what of the role.

- The Role Clarity Map brings fresh perspective to the Heroic Question— *Is it actionable?*
- Helps you notice opportunities, increasing your return on luck.
- Shapes the future promises and agreements you make with yourself and others, building confidence and trust.

Identify roles, draft your story, create clarity, and build momentum.

Let's build a role together.

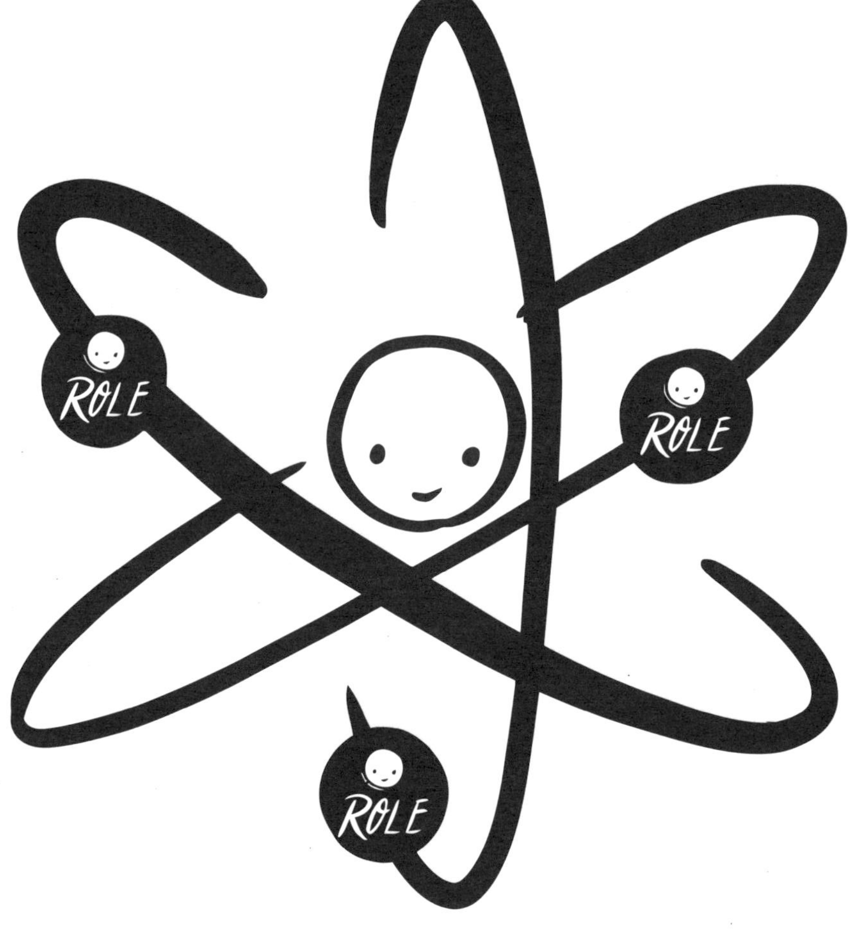
ROLE
ROLE
ROLE

# Roles Are Dynamic

Life is dynamic and so are you. Here are the five types of roles you will experience over the arc of your life.

- **Anchor Role**: This is your *me* role. It holds your core purpose for life.
- **Current Roles**: These roles hold a majority of your current reality. Common examples: daughter, son; sister, brother, family; wife, husband, partner; mother, father, parent; work, job, business owner; caregiver.
- **Temporary Roles**: This type of role holds your short-term and unexpected roles. Examples: participating in a year-long executive training program, starting a short-term hobby, engaging in a job search, taking a sabbatical.
- **Emerging Roles**: These are roles that are unfolding. They create space for new opportunities and possibilities. Examples: If you want to be a writer, create a role called *writer*. If you want a side-hustle business, create a role called *Side-hustle*.
- **Past Roles**: These are roles that are done. They are in the past. Example: When you graduate, you're a former student.

Roles puts confidence in your choices and purpose in your actions.

- **P** — Purpose (Why)
- **V** — Vision
- **Role**
- **Pr** — Practices
- **Pj** — Projects (How)
- **A** — Actions (What)

# Parts of a Role

There are six parts to a role.

The name:
- Role Name

Why parts:
- Purpose
- Vision

The how parts:
- Practices
- Projects

The what part:
- Actions

With the help of our everyday heroes, let's show examples of each.

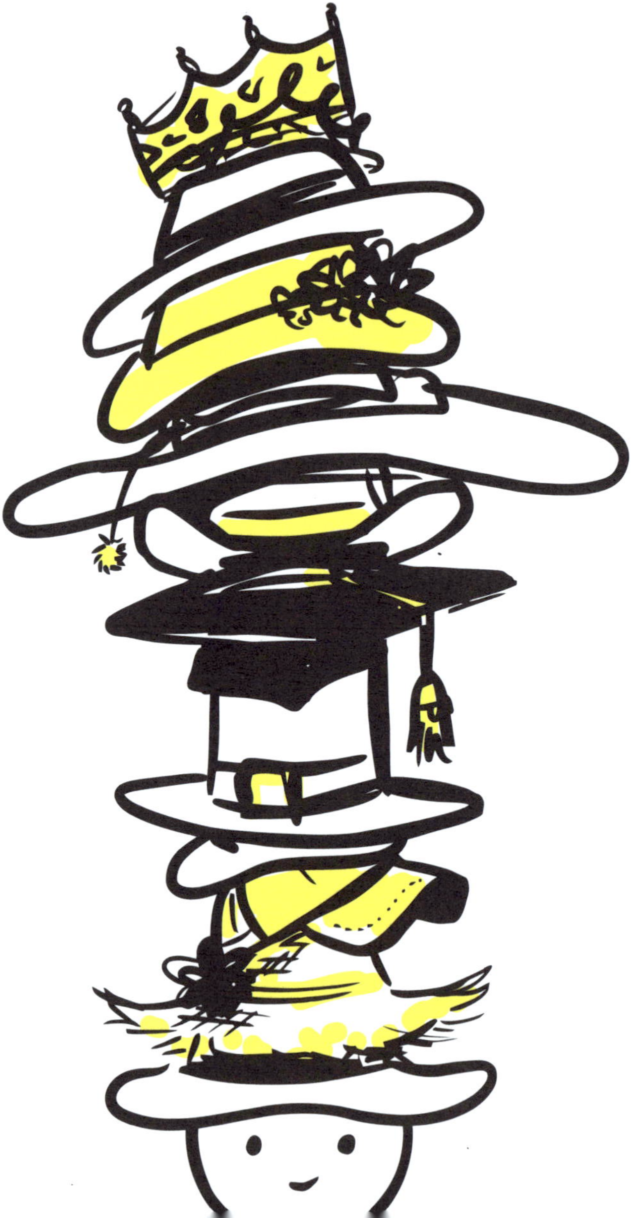

# Role Name

When you name a role, you claim it and give it room to evolve. Here are some examples:

- ***Conrad's roles***: Conrad, Son/Brother/Family, Boyfriend, Friends, College Student (Communications, 3D Art, Art History, Drawing), Work, Surfer.
- ***Hannah's roles***: Me, Daughter/Sister, Family, Girlfriend, Roommate, Work (Social Media Strategist, Project Manager, Employee), Clothing Brand Side Hustle.
- ***Keri's roles***: Me, Actor, Work (Founder, Manager, Creative Director, Lead Copywriter), Friend & Family Member, Homeowner, Cat Mother, Community.
- ***Jeff's roles***: Me, Husband/Father, Family/Friends, Work (Leader, Coach, Marketing Leadership Team Member, Sport Advocate, Product Advisor), Volleyball Coach, Board Member, Golf for Joy.
- ***Gina's roles***: This Is Gina! Wife/Mom, Family/Close Friends, Homeschool Teacher, Doctor, Musician, Teacher.
- ***Maggie's roles***: Me, Mom, Family/Friends, Step-Mom, Community Member, Community Builder, Consultant.

Roles come in all shapes and sizes.

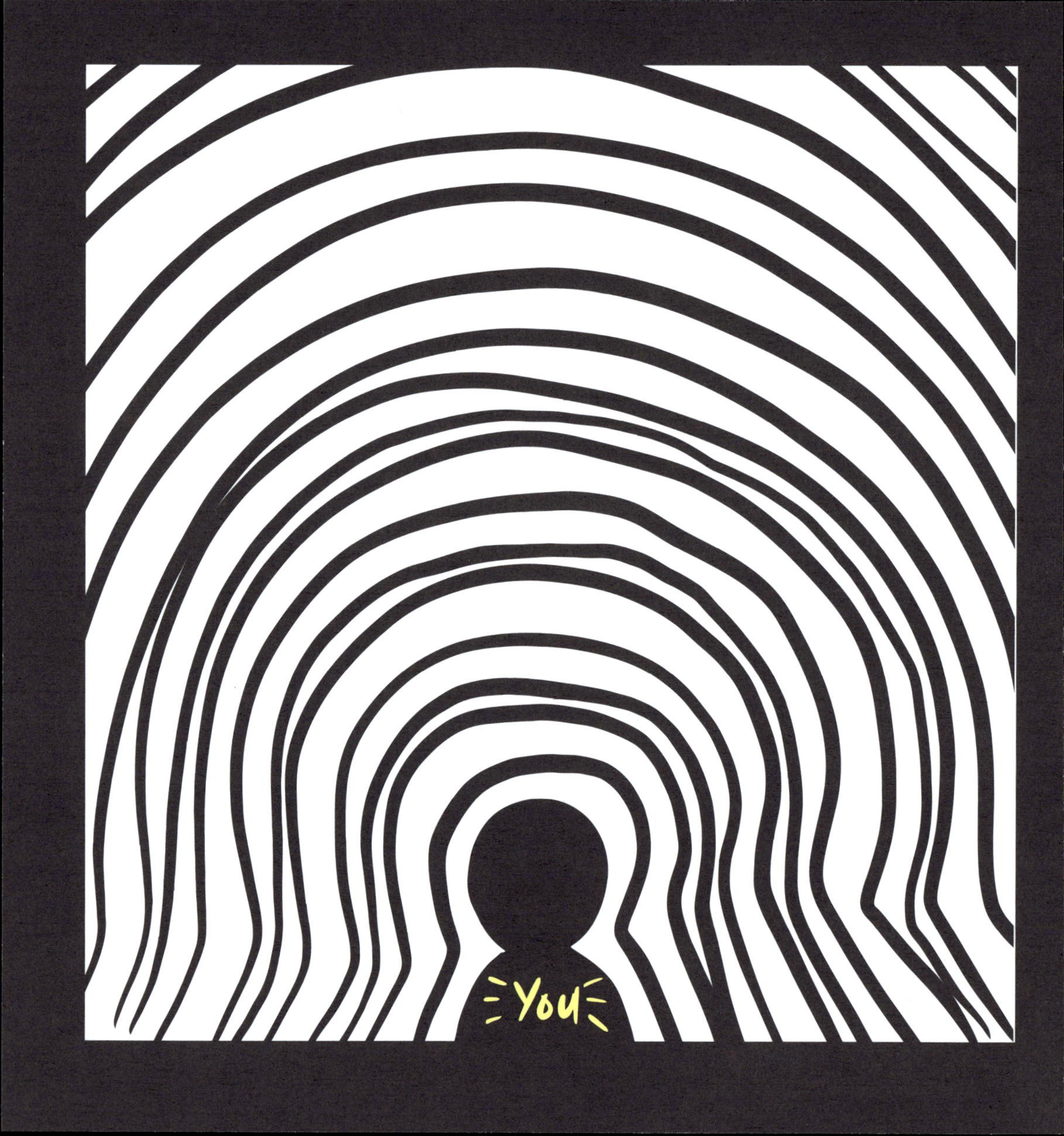
You

# Purpose

A purpose statement holds the contribution you seek to make. A role always has a purpose, whether implicit or explicit. Purpose statements are succinct yet hold a bold intention. They have two common forms:

1. To ***contribution***.
2. To ***contribution*** so ***that impact***.

Here are a few examples by role:

- Gina's "This is Gina!" role: *To share cross-pollinating ideas that inspire others to learn and grow.*
- Keri's Actor role: *To play big with my performing so that I can reach a bigger audience, thereby spreading joy and encouraging others on a larger scale.*
- Jeff's Husband/Father role: *To create the conditions for our family to be in the zone of life, share love and experiences, and stay connected.*
- Keri's Lead Copywriter role: *To oversee all outward facing copy so that the brand voice remains consistent across all platforms.*
- Jeff's Golf for Joy role: *To enjoy being outdoors, pushing myself to progress and enjoy golf even more.*

A distinct purpose puts vital energy into your role.

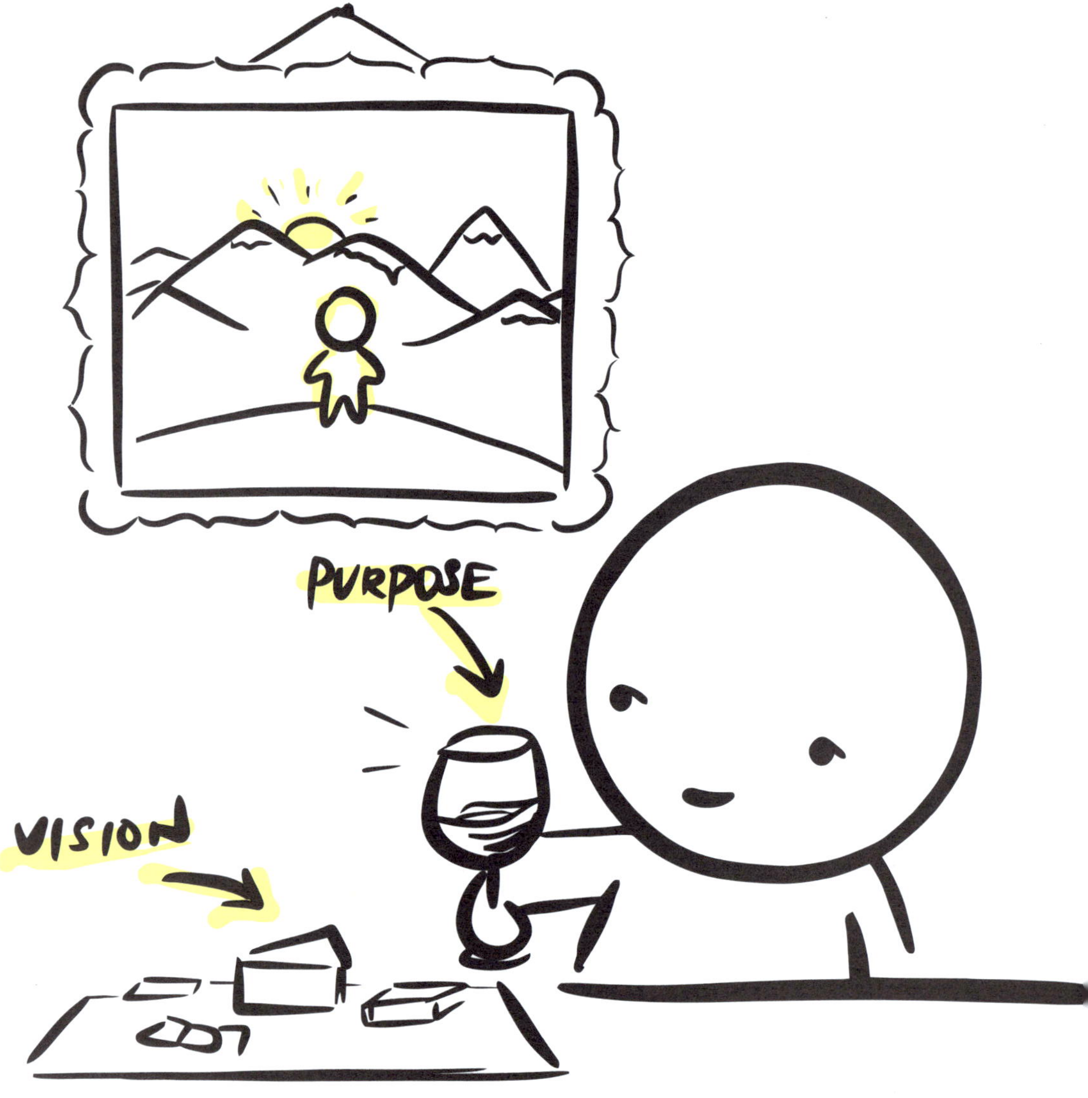
PURPOSE
VISION

# Vision

Picture what success looks, sounds, and feels like for this role. What do you see?

For your vision, find, make, or draw a picture that represents your definition of wild success for this role.

Why a picture? A picture is truly worth a thousand words. It engages the visual part of your brain, infusing the role with more meaning than words alone can hold.

Like in a photo album, the pictures you look at are the stories you practice. The stories you practice get strengthened.

A few words and an image are all it takes to amplify your intention and improve your recall.

Your purpose (text) and vision (image) make a perfect pair, like wine and cheese.

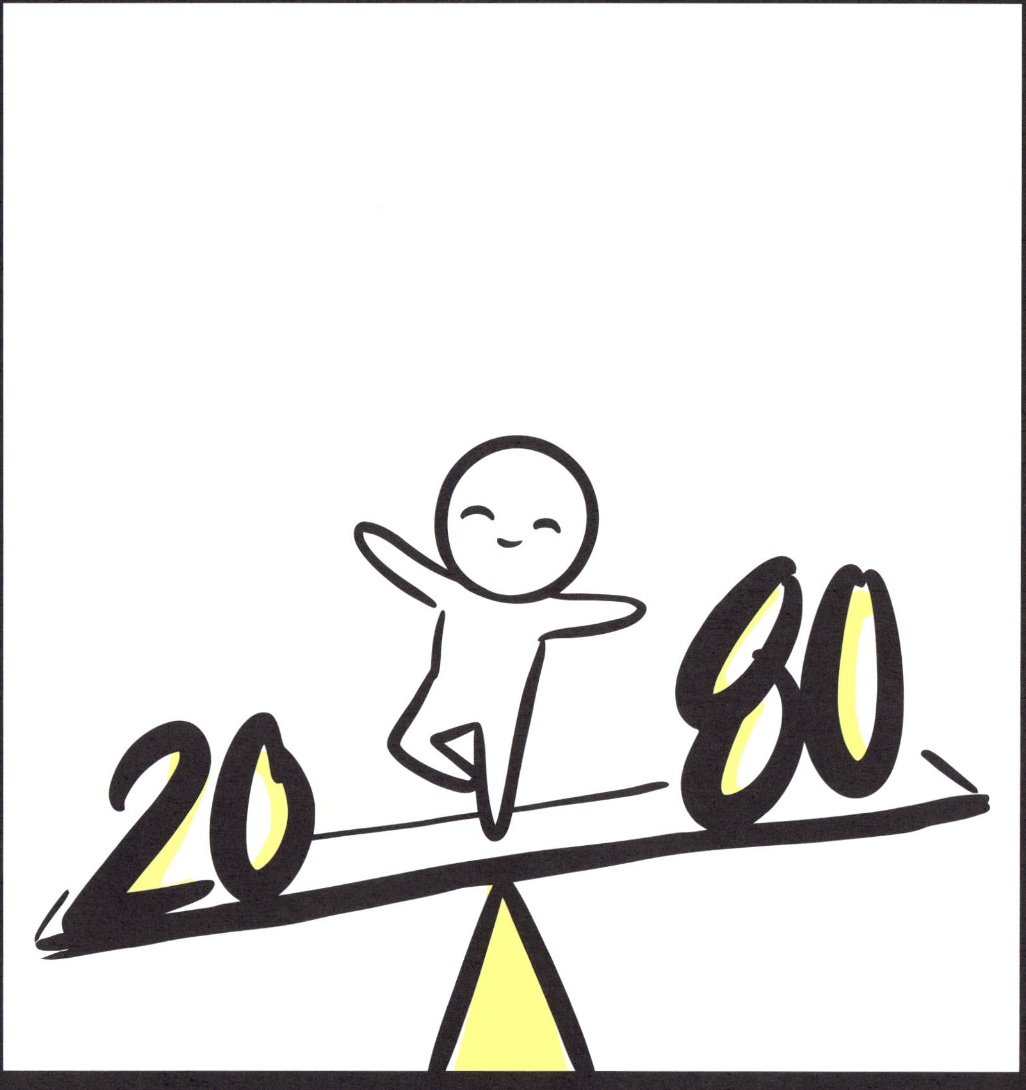
20
80

# Practices

Practices are routines that help you improve. In business, they're called processes.

The aim here is to list the one to three practices that create a majority of the value for a role—the 20/80 rule.

Here are a few examples by role:

- In Keri's Actor role, her practice for managing the business side of acting is to have a conversation with her accountability partner using a checklist she created.
- In Conrad's Student role, his practice is to run through his weekly review checklist with a friend to stay on top of his assignments and projects.
- In Jeff's Golf for Joy role, his practices are backyard practice, range practice, and playing rounds of golf.
- In Maggie's Me role, she practices the Happy Body routine to maintain her wellness.
- In Hannah's Social Media Strategist role, she stays on top of her game by updating her social media content calendar weekly.

What practices, if done consistently, will help you thrive?

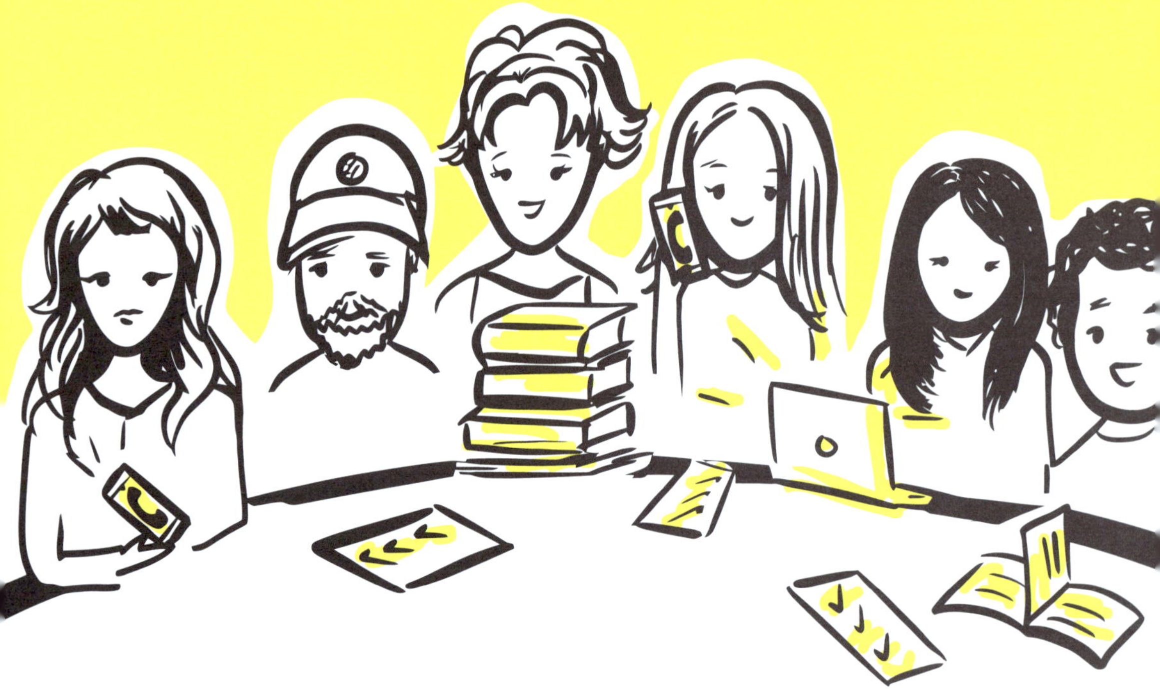

# Projects and Actions

Projects are the second type of how. A project is about creating something new or implementing a change, whereas a practice creates value through repetition. A project has a defined beginning and end. Project statements describe done.

Action statements describe the next action—*doing*.

Here are a few examples by role:

- In Conrad's Student role, Project: *Fall class registration completed*. Action: *Review major requirements, select classes*.
- In Hannah's Roommate role, Project: *Apartment decorated*. Action: *Buy coffee table*.
- In Keri's Actor role, Project: *Actor website updated*. Action: *Get web designer recommendation from Barret*.
- In Jeff's Volleyball Coaching role, Project: *Volleyball tryouts completed*. Action: *Email final team roster*.
- In Gina's Teacher role, Project: *Fall semester completed*. Action: *Order books*.
- In Maggie's family role, Project: *Dad's estate resolved*. Action: *Schedule call with sister*.

One by one, projects and actions help you embody your purpose and vision.

**These heroes are on a journey.**

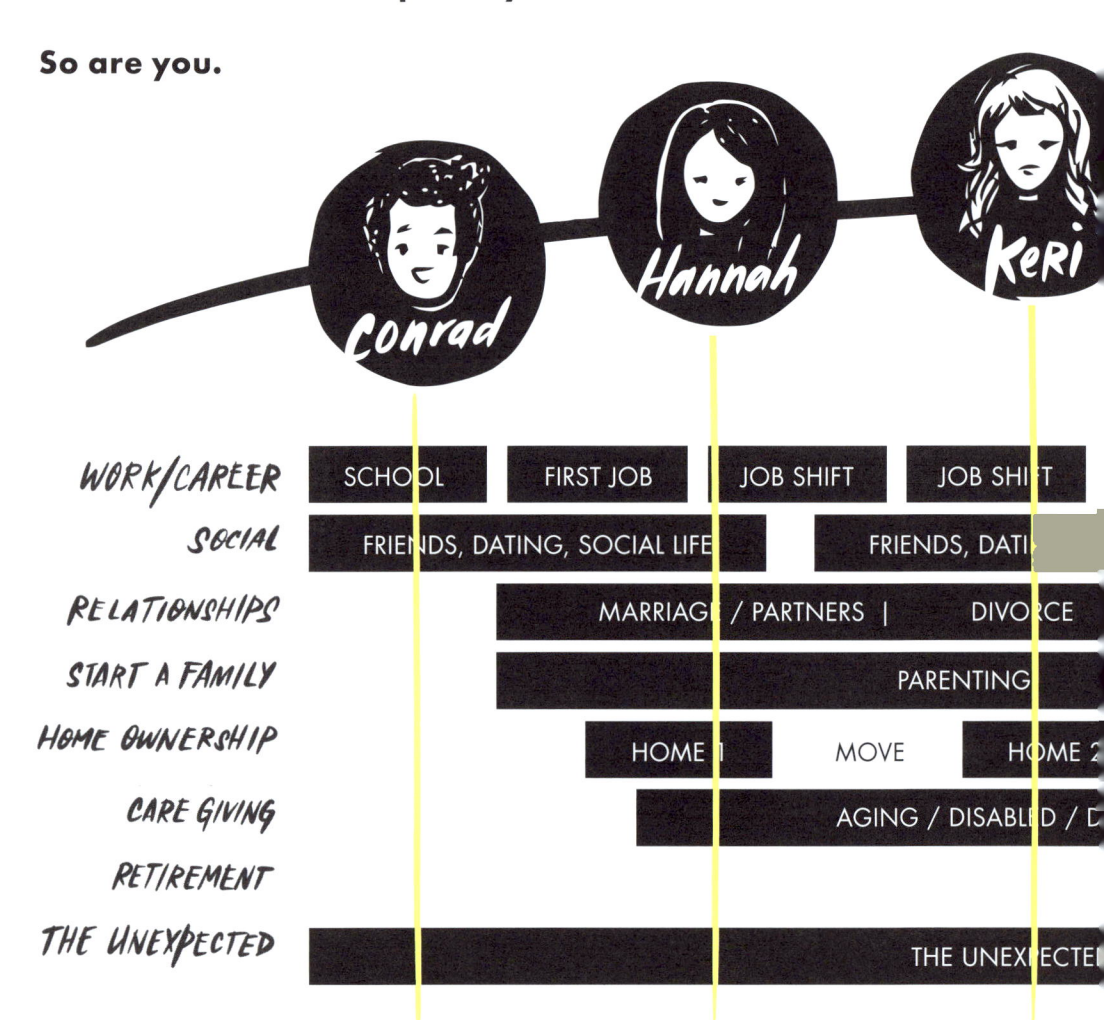

**So are you.**

- Conrad
- Hannah
- Keri

| | | | | |
|---|---|---|---|---|
| WORK/CAREER | SCHOOL | FIRST JOB | JOB SHIFT | JOB SHIFT |
| SOCIAL | FRIENDS, DATING, SOCIAL LIFE | | FRIENDS, DATI... | |
| RELATIONSHIPS | | MARRIAGE / PARTNERS | | DIVORCE |
| START A FAMILY | | | PARENTING | |
| HOME OWNERSHIP | | HOME 1 | MOVE | HOME 2 |
| CARE GIVING | | | AGING / DISABLED / D... | |
| RETIREMENT | | | | |
| THE UNEXPECTED | | | | THE UNEXPECTE... |

## Where are you on life's journey?

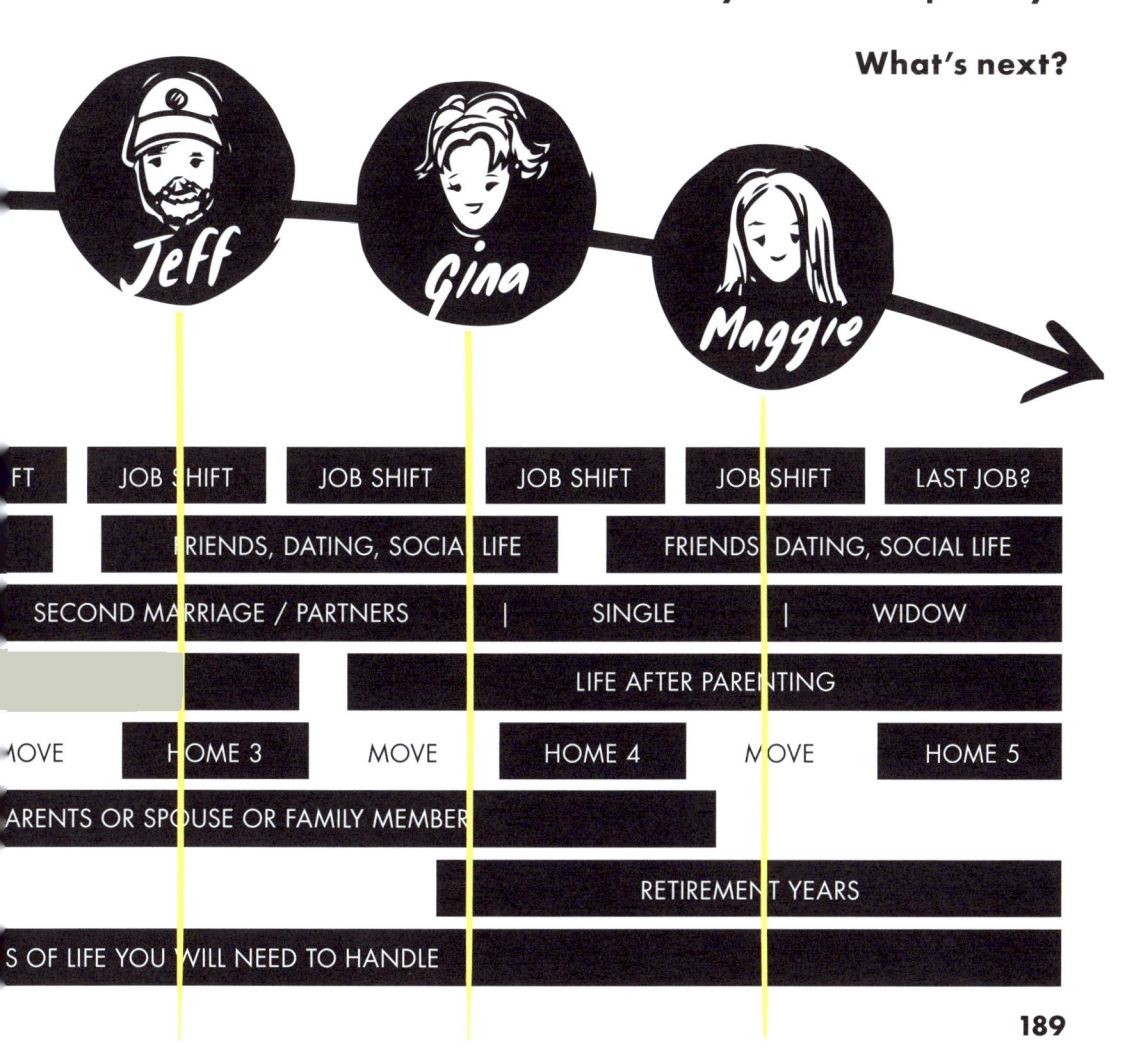

### What's next?

**Jeff** — **Gina** — **Maggie**

| | | | | | |
|---|---|---|---|---|---|
| FT | JOB SHIFT | JOB SHIFT | JOB SHIFT | JOB SHIFT | LAST JOB? |

FRIENDS, DATING, SOCIAL LIFE — FRIENDS, DATING, SOCIAL LIFE

SECOND MARRIAGE / PARTNERS | SINGLE | WIDOW

LIFE AFTER PARENTING

MOVE — HOME 3 — MOVE — HOME 4 — MOVE — HOME 5

ARENTS OR SPOUSE OR FAMILY MEMBER

RETIREMENT YEARS

S OF LIFE YOU WILL NEED TO HANDLE

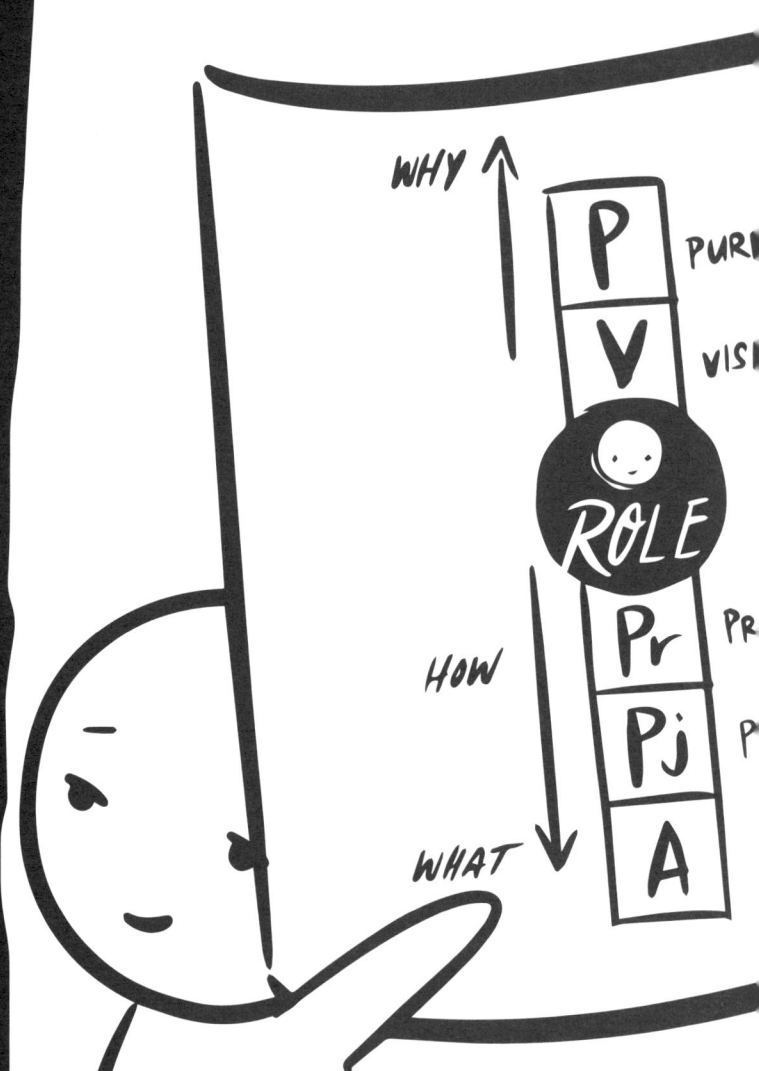

# YOUR ROLE CLARITY MAP

| ME | ROLE | ROLE | ROLE | ROLE | ROLE | ROLE | ROLE | ROLE |
|---|---|---|---|---|---|---|---|---|

"WHERE ARE YOU ON LIFE'S JOURNEY? WHAT'S NEXT?"

# Recap

## Key Terms
- Roles
- The Role Clarity Map
- The why direction: Purpose, Vision
- The who/what directions: Practices, Projects, Actions
- Five types of roles: Anchor, Current, Temporary, Emerging, Past

## Key Questions
- What are your roles?
- Will you define and activate any new roles?
- Any roles to let go?

## Job it does
- Names your roles, creating clarity.
- Defines your intentions.
- Puts inspiration and purpose into your practices, projects, and actions.

## Key Ideas
- You're a wonderfully complex human being. Your roles change and shift as you move through life. The Role Clarity Map helps you find and fulfill your calling in life, through all stages of life.

# YOUR TRUSTED SYSTEM MAP

YOUR ROLE CLARITY MAP

⭐ SWEEP IT

⭐ TRANSFORM IT

YOUR PROJECT CLARITY MAP
WHAT DOES DOING LOOK LIKE?
WHAT DOES DONE LOOK LIKE?
REVIEW IT
DO IT

# Build Your Trusted System

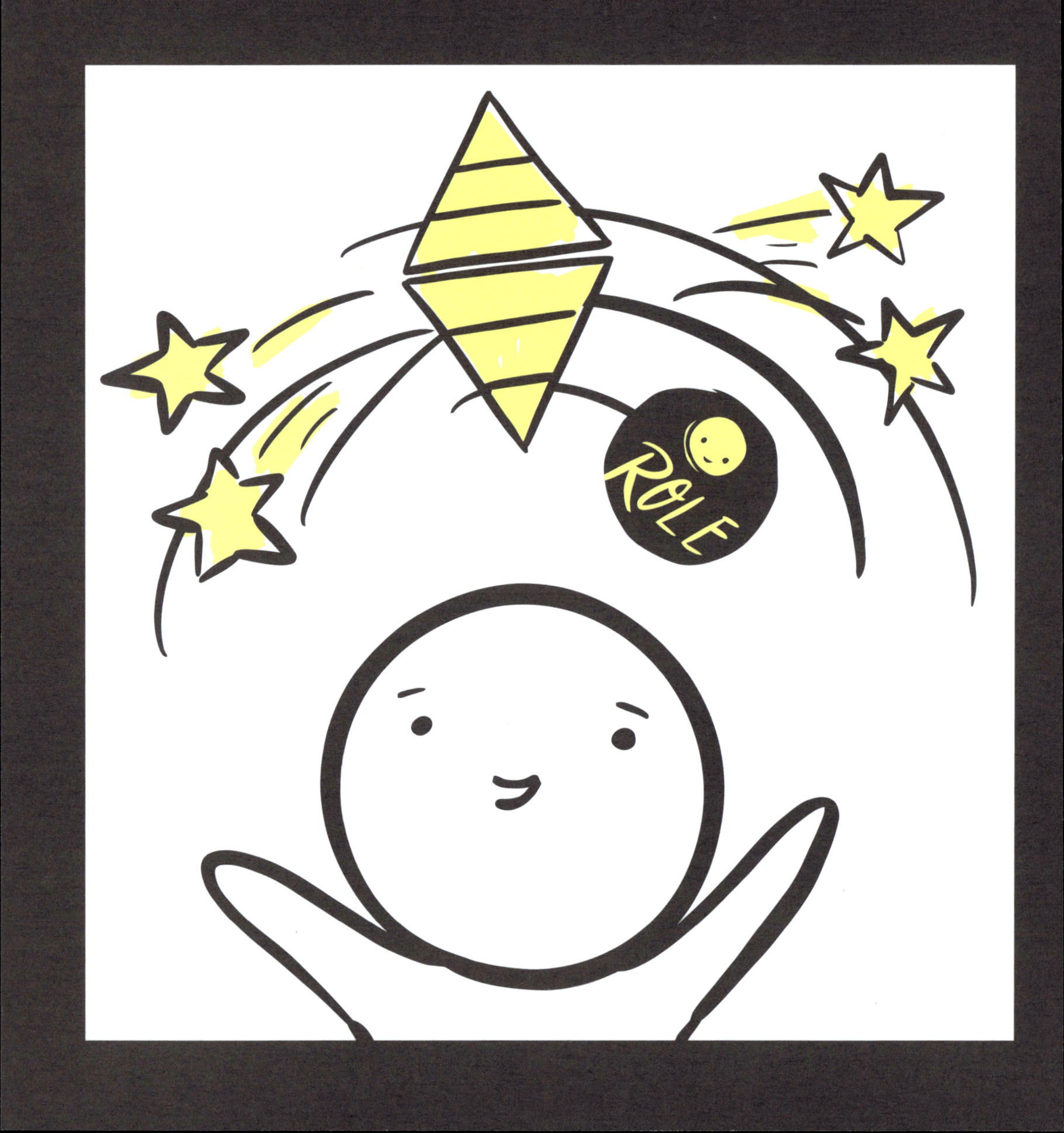
ROLE

# Build Your Trusted System

Building your trusted system is like designing the house of your dreams—your sanctuary for insight, revelations, and inspiration.

You have the core know-how to build your trusted system.

- The Four Repeatable Wins
- The Role Clarity Map
- The Project Clarity Map

Let's build it.

Like building a house, there are small design decisions to make along the way as you build your Action and Storage Systems.

You have three main approaches: paper-based, digital, blended. Starting with the most common, let's build a digital system that works seamlessly across all your devices.

Build your trusted system in a few easy steps; set yourself up for lifelong success.

# Library of Examples

Oh, the joy! You know, the thrill you get when you flip through your favorite catalog of gizmos and gadgets, or walk through your favorite specialty store, or touch samples of swatches? It's so delightful.

Examples are playful, joyful, and informative—they stir your imagination.

Productivity principles endure. But you've probably noticed the tools change and evolve, which is a blessing and a curse. It can be a challenge to sort through it all.

No problem, got you covered.

Through the magic of QR codes, this book grows with you.

As you read this section, hover over the QR codes in the illustrations with your camera app. You'll get additional tips, stories, and micro-lessons to help you build Your Trusted System.

Explore possibilities. Set yourself up for wild success today—and the future.

# Build Your Action System

First step, let's build your trusted Action System.

Based on my years of teaching and coaching, I discovered people have enduring success when selecting productivity software that matches these three criteria.

- Criteria 1: Does it work across your mobile, web, tablet, and computer?
- Criteria 2: Can you easily organize your work into roles, projects, actions?
- Criteria 3: Can you create three types of views with the click of a button?
    - List of projects with actions
    - List of actions with projects
    - List of actions by user-defined tags

Follow the QR code to get a current list of recommended software applications for your Action System, including a simple, elegant, and powerful solution I use with a majority of my clients.

# Role, Project, Action

There's power in simplicity. Same is true for your Action System. The *Role-Project-Action* is a simple form that puts you in the driver's seat of your life.

### *Role-Name*
- Project Name (What does done look like?)
  - Action Name (What does doing look like?)

### *Role-Team Leader*
- Annual performance reviews completed *(Done)*
  - Schedule slots for all team members *(Doing)*
- Next year's budget approved *(Done)*
  - Email team to get budget requests *(Doing)*

### *Role-Parent*
- Summer camps for kids scheduled *(Done)*
  - Text mom group for ideas *(Doing)*
- Create trust/will for family *(Done)*
  - Check benefit portal for legal services *(Doing)*

Follow the QR code to see more **Role-Project-Action** examples to inspire you as you build your Action System.

# Build Your Storage System

Like your Action System, your Storage System is simple by design. Find and retrieve information with minimum effort and maximum speed. You'll impress yourself, friends, and coworkers.

You'll need two things:
- Storage area 1: You need a place to store lists.
- Storage area 2: You need a place to store reference material and information.

In the digital realm, it's as simple as creating two folders:
- Folder 1: List of Lists
- Folder 2: Reference

I highly recommend you select a digital storage solution that allows you to create links to your files and folders.

For your physical reference, a file cabinet with your files sorted from A to Z does the trick.

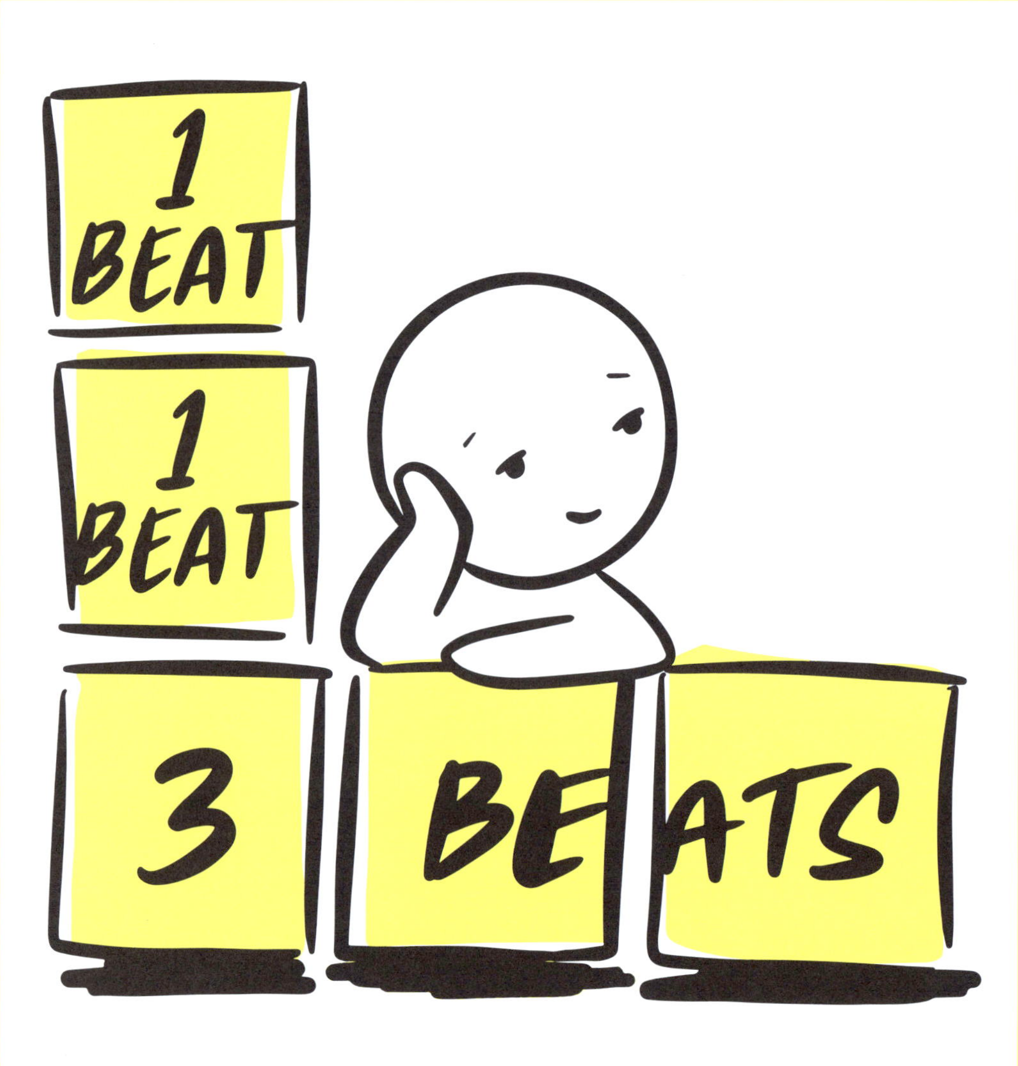
1 BEAT
1 BEAT
3
BEATS

# Build Your Keystone Work Beats

At the summit of a stone arch, there is a central stone that holds everything together—the keystone.

Your trusted system has three keystone work beats. These beats, **_In-Do-Win_** moments, put creativity, confidence, and joy into your day.

Brain Sweep + Transform It—Creates clarity (1 beat).
Do It—Do one action to create momentum (1 beat).
Weekly Review, Reflect, Reset—Creates perspective (3 beats).

Do these three work beats regularly; make them a habit; everything else locks into place.

Win small. Win big.

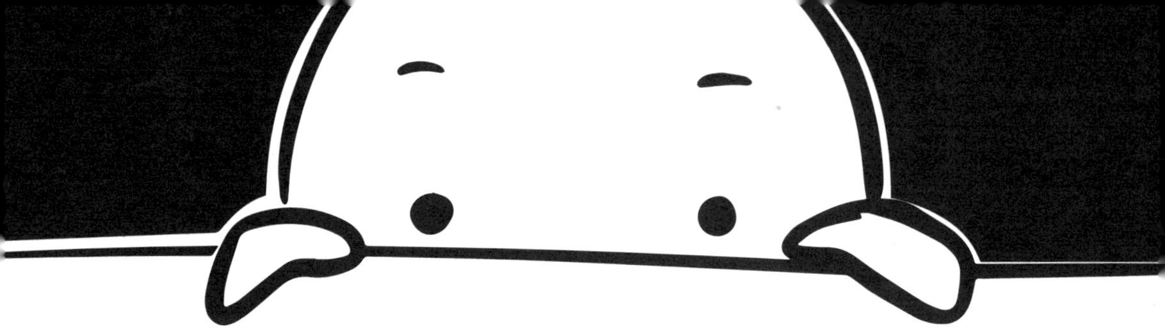

# Inaugural Projects

Drum roll please...you're ready to get started. Let's turn your implementation into a series of small projects so you can win, win, and win some more! Use Your Trusted System to create Your Trusted System—so meta!

Here's a list of inaugural projects needed to create the first version of Your Trusted System. How exciting! Let's get you set up for success.

- Role: Me
  - Project: First draft of Role Clarity Map (role names only) completed.
  - Project: Action System set up.
  - Project: Storage System set up.
  - Project: First Doing to Done week completed.
  - Project: First Doing to Done month completed.

Of course, remember to enter these projects into your Action System.

# Your First Week

Week 1: Goal—build momentum with small wins. Your keystone work beats lead the way. Win the moment, win the day, win the week—with this proven jump-start plan.

Daily practices:
- **Brain Sweep + Transform It** (*1 beat*). Creates clarity.
  - Schedule a daily time; show up for your date with yourself. (*In*)
  - Use a timer, Brain Sweep for 5 minutes. Transform your Brain Sweep for 10 minutes. (*Do*)
  - Stop. Notice what has your attention and the clarity you created. (*Win!*)

- **Do It** (*1 beat*). Creates momentum.
  - Select one next action from your Action list. (*In*)
  - Use a timer, work on the action for 15-minutes or less. (*Do*)
  - Stop. Notice your clarity of action, alignment, and momentum. (*Win!*)

Weekly practice:
- **Weekly—Review It** (*3 beats*). Creates perspective.
  - Schedule a weekly time; show up for your date with yourself. (*In*)
  - Use a timer, Review, Reflect, Reset—one beat each. (*Do*)
  - Stop. Notice your perspective, your ability to create a fresh start. (*Win!*)

# Your First Month

With your first week completed, your foundation is sound, trust is growing, and momentum is building. Here's the plan for your first month.

Week 1:
- Complete the three keystone work beats.

Week 2:
- Complete the three keystone work beats.
- Update #2 to the Role Clarity Map (add purpose and vision).
- Key experience: Create your first Project Clarity Map.

Week 3:
- Complete the three keystone work beats.
- Update #3 to the Role Clarity Map (add practices).
- Key experience: Get your Yesterbox to zero.

Week 4:
- Complete the three keystone work beats.

Consistent small wins, weekly fresh starts, create new possibilities.

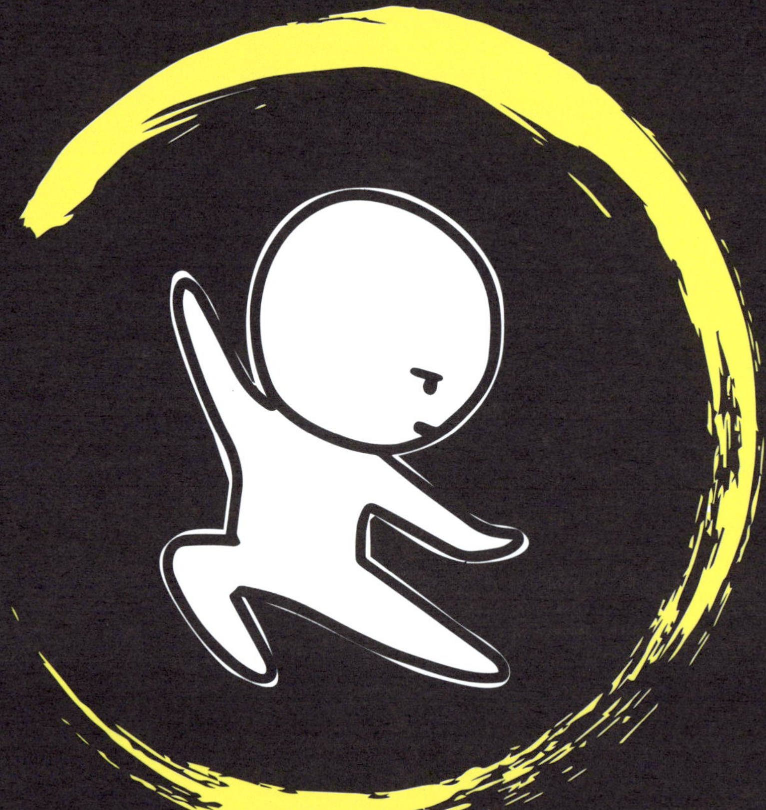

# The Art of Imperfectivity

There's a Japanese aesthetic called wabi-sabi. It points to a beauty of things imperfect, impermanent, and incomplete; the beauty of things modest and humble; the beauty of things unconventional.

As you build and use your Trusted System, I invite you to be imperfect, unique, and unconventional. My name for this is *imperfectivity*.

As I work with my clients, and we encounter the Heroic Question (*Is it actionable?*), we untangle all types of stuff. I often find myself sharing the story of wabi-sabi.

### Be kind to yourself.

You're wabi-sabi—perfect in your imperfectivity.

"YOUR TRUSTED SYSTEM... YOUR SANCTUARY FOR INSIGHTS, REVELATIONS, AND INSPIRATIONS."

# Recap

## Key Terms
- Your Trusted System
- Your Trusted Action System
- Your Trusted Storage System
- Role-Project-Action
- Inaugural projects
- Your First Week
- Your First Month

## Key Ideas
- Consistent small wins, weekly fresh starts, create new possibilities.
- As you build and use your trusted system, be imperfect, unique, and unconventional.

## Tip
- Use the QR codes to get additional tips, stories, and micro-lessons to help you build your Trusted System.

# Land of Possibilities

# Your Fresh Start

Small wins. Big impacts. It's that simple.

Your Trusted System is all about gaining simple, repeatable wins that help you stay present, productive, and ready for anything life throws your way.

Welcome to the LAND of POSSIB

LITIES

# Thank You

- Kristine Yan, who knew altMBA #33 would lead us here? Thanks for your friendship, artistic vision, overflowing goodness. You're amazing!
- Deep gratitude to Maggie Weiss, Monica Russell, Adam Wayne, and Chrissa Trudelle for the hours of insightful conversation, edits, and friendship; thanks to Brad and Anna Swonetz, Gillian Griffith, and Adam Bucci for your friendship and creative support; a big thank you to all my beta readers.
- The lineage of Doing to Done comes from many mentors who have influenced and encouraged me throughout the years. Specifically, David Allen (my productivity mentor), Dan Roam (my visual thinking mentor), and Charles Fred (my Speed-to-Proficiency mentor).
- A big thank you to the communities that nurtured me and influenced this book: Seth Godin's Akimbo community (altMBA #33, the Story Skills Workshop); Stephen Kotler and the Flow for Writers community; the Ferguson's Airstream community; Zappos, Life Is Beautiful and DTLV community; ATD.org board of directors and global talent development community; the Conrad Challenge and The Knowledge Society (TKS).
- A very special thank you to my clients, customers, and partners throughout the years, with a special heartfelt nod to Stephen Lease and the goodr team, Jeff Boliba, Keri Blunt, Gina Lokna, Andy Armstrong, Danielle Houle, Jason Spafford, and Stephan Mardyks.

- And my deepest thank you to Hannah and Conrad, and to the love of my life, Arianna Williams—thank you for helping me turn our experience at Table #3 into an unforeseen happy ending!

# There's No Better Time Than Now.

# Let's Do This.

There's a better way (read: way better). I'm here to help you tame the chaos and manage the complexities of business and life with ease—so you (your team, your company) can stay relaxed and ready for anything the world throws your way. Step one? That starts right here.

For more information about joining an online workshop, hosting a company event, or scheduling private coaching visit: **doingtodone.com/next**.

Productivity Made Simple.

# Notes

# Notes

# Notes

# Notes

# Notes

# Notes